SIN

Sin

GREGORY MELLEMA

University of Notre Dame Press
Notre Dame, Indiana

Published in the United States of America

Library of Congress Control Number: 2021941558

ISBN: 978-0-268-20133-3 (Hardback)
ISBN: 978-0-268-20132-6 (WebPDF)
ISBN: 978-0-268-20135-7 (Epub)

To my youngest grandchildren

Tinsley Elise Thomas
Quinn Rosaleigh Thomas

CONTENTS

Preface ix
Acknowledgments xv

ONE   Original and Inherited Sin   1

TWO   Individual and Collective Sins   11

THREE   Accessory Sins   21

FOUR   Mortal versus Venial Sins   31

FIVE   Supererogation and Sin   41

SIX   The Islamic Category of Acts That Are Discouraged   53

SEVEN   Moral Ideals, Virtue Ethics, and Sin   63

EIGHT   Sin and Symbolism   73

NINE   Sin and the Problem of Evil   87

TEN   Sin in Six Major World Religions   95

Notes   103
Bibliography   105
Index   111

PREFACE

Most of the scholarly literature on sin has focused on theological issues or questions of scriptural interpretation. Philosophical treatments of sin have been less than abundant and have mostly taken the form of articles in scholarly journals or book chapters. My belief is that a useful purpose can be served by a book-length treatment of philosophical issues concerning sin. Among other things, this volume brings together contributions by such philosophers as Marilyn Adams, Robert Adams, Rebecca DeYoung, Alvin Plantinga, Michael Rea, Eleonore Stump, and Richard Swinburne into a coherent discussion that has the potential to clarify our understanding of the nature of sin. This treatment will focus on moral issues; there will be occasional forays into issues of the epistemology and philosophy of religion, but the overall theme of the book can be described as sin and moral wrongdoing.

Chapter 1 deals with sin as a fundamental feature of the human condition that is permanent and inescapable. According to this usage, "sin" functions as a mass term, a term that does not admit of pluralization. Here various traditional views as to the nature of sin will be examined and evaluated. For example, original sin, especially the Augustinian account of original sin, refers to the effect on humanity caused by the sinful behavior of the first human beings while living in paradise. Many have held that original sin has epistemological consequences, often referred to as the noetic (intellectual) effects of sin. Others, such as Leibniz, have discussed whether this doctrine is unfair to those of us who suffer the effects of sin that are not of our own making. Primal sin refers to the effect on humanity caused by the alleged rebellion of certain angels, an event that took place before human beings came into existence.

Chapter 2 is a survey of reasons that people have offered for how actions acquire the status of sinful actions. First, a sinful action is one that violates moral duty or obligation. Second, a sinful action is one that is worthy of moral blame. Third, a sinful action is one for which guilt is an appropriate response. Fourth, a sinful action is one that is offensive or displeasing to a particular deity. A remedy for sin of the fourth type is illustrated by the account of scapegoats in the Book of Leviticus. The Day of Atonement is described in terms of a priest laying his hands on the head of a goat and the goat's subsequently being driven into the wilderness. It was believed that the sins of the people had been laid on the goat and were removed from the people into the wilderness. The second part of this chapter defends the claim that in some instances sense can be made of the assertion that a sin has been committed by a group or collective. Likewise, sense can be made of the assertion that a group or collective can bear guilt (popularly known as "collective guilt") for having committed such a sin.

The next two chapters are concerned with accessory sins and the distinction between cardinal sins and venial sins. The medievals spoke a great deal about accessory sins, sins whereby one is complicit in the wrongdoing of another. In chapter 3 the nine accessory sins presented by Thomas Aquinas will be identified and examined. Thereafter I take up the modern notion of complicity and discuss ways in which one can avoid becoming complicit in the sinful acts of another. In the final section I will examine moral luck in relation to the avoidance of becoming complicit in the sinful actions of another.

The Roman Catholic Church has for centuries maintained that a distinction can be drawn between mortal (or cardinal) sins and venial sins. In this way of thinking, some sins are more serious than others. Chapter 4 will begin with an in-depth examination of the distinction between mortal sins and venial sins. The next section will explore the broader position that some sins are more serious than others from a moral point of view. In addition, I will discuss the possibility that this point of view may motivate some individuals to minimize the gravity or seriousness of certain kinds of sin. The final section addresses the topic of the seven deadly sins, including the historical progression by which the tradition of identifying these sins evolved.

Chapter 5 deals with the topic of supererogation. An act of supererogation is defined as an act that is morally praiseworthy to perform but not morally obligatory to perform and not morally blameworthy to omit. Since the time of the Reformation there has been a good deal of opposition to the possibility of supererogation on the grounds that every act that is praiseworthy to perform is also obligatory to perform. In other words, many have held that whenever we have an opportunity to do something praiseworthy, we have a corresponding obligation to do so.

The relevance of sin to the discussion of supererogation can be captured (in part) by these questions: If human beings are as sinful as they appear to be, is it ever possible for them to go beyond the call of duty? Can it ever be sinful to refrain intentionally from going beyond the call of duty? I answer both questions in the affirmative. Even if human beings suffer from original sin, they can and do at times act so as to transcend the boundaries of duty. And refraining from an act of supererogation as the result of a vicious motive can qualify as sinful.

Islamic codes of ethics include a category of acts that are "discouraged." Chapter 6 explores the relevance of this category to other moral concepts and categories and to sin in particular. Julia Driver has identified a category of acts, the suberogatory, that she believes comes close to capturing the essence of this Islamic category. In addition, the commands of God can be distinguished from the expectations of God, and I argue that failing to do what God expects but does not require or doing what God expects us not to do but does not forbid can frequently qualify as acts that are discouraged. In the final section I explain the relevance of the preceding discussion to sin.

Chapter 7 takes up the topic of moral ideals. That which is ideal is sometimes characterized as that which is devoid of sin, and consequently the sinful actions of human beings are sometimes thought of in terms of the failure to achieve ideals, moral ideals in particular. A key manner of attaining moral ideals, I urge, comes by way of practicing moral virtue. Therefore, sin can take the form of the failure to develop moral virtue, the intent to develop moral vice, or simply the practice of moral vice.

The symbolic dimension of sin is the subject matter of chapter 8. The symbolism of sin is a familiar notion. The color red is sometimes said to symbolize sin (as in Isaiah 1:18, "Though your sins be as scarlet . . ."), and symbolism of this type can be helpful in understanding the nature of sin. However, in this chapter I will present a concept of symbolism derived from the work of Robert Nozick that will allow us to understand the symbolism of sin on a deeper level. His notion of the symbolic value of an act is the idea that the performance of one act can symbolize the performance of other actual or potential acts or states of affairs in a manner that has moral significance. The first section of this chapter will present Nozick's notion of symbolic value and explain how it contributes to our understanding of virtue ethics. The second section illustrates the application of this notion to sin or, more specifically, sins that take the form of vice. The final section broadens the discussion to the consideration of group behavior.

The relationship between sin and evil is sometimes stated succinctly as follows: All sin is evil, but not all evil is sin (the suffering caused by a natural disaster, for example). One fruitful way to gain a greater depth of understanding of how sin and evil are related is to analyze the so-called problem of evil. The first section of chapter 9 explains how J. L. Mackie articulates the problem of evil. The second section examines the role sin has played in the literature on the problem of evil, most notably Alvin Plantinga's free will defense.

The concluding chapter focuses on sin as it is understood in the context of major world religions. It examines the teachings of six world religions: Catholicism, Hinduism, Islam, Judaism, Orthodoxy, and Protestantism (Buddhist thought has no concept of sin comparable to what is understood by the other six religions). I will analyze certain of these teachings against the backdrop of the previous nine chapters. The final section of this chapter will contain concluding comments for the book as a whole.

From the foregoing chapter summaries it is perhaps obvious that the concept of sin is multifaceted. The relationship between sin and moral wrongdoing is complex and resists summarization in a sentence or two, and I will not attempt to offer a definition of sin that stipulates necessary and sufficient conditions. A related point: This book does not take the form of a single, sustained line of argument developed over the course of multiple chapters. Rather, each chapter addresses a particular topic and contains arguments appropriate to its subject matter. If there is a single overarching link among the ten chapters, it is that the topic of sin is fundamentally connected to the subject matter of morality. I believe that analyzing these points of connection is profitable not just to enhance our theoretical understanding of sin but to give us a greater depth of knowledge as to how the moral choices we make can more effectively avoid sin and contribute to lives that are satisfying and authentically worthwhile.

ACKNOWLEDGMENTS

Portions of chapter 8 appeared in *Philosophy Today* 43 (1999), no. 3, 302–308. I thank the editor for permission to include this material.

I am grateful to two anonymous readers for a number of extensive helpful criticisms and advice.

CHAPTER ONE

ORIGINAL AND INHERITED SIN

This chapter concerns sin when it is taken to be a fundamental feature of the human condition. Understood in this manner, sin is not considered to be a property of people's individual actions; rather, it is understood to be a property of the human condition in general.

The most popular version of the idea that sin is a pervasive feature of the human condition is the doctrine of original sin and, in particular, the Augustinian account of original sin. The first section of this chapter surveys how this doctrine has been understood by various philosophers and by various religious traditions. The second section takes up the question of the noetic effects of sin. The third section deals with the question of whether the doctrine of original sin is unfair or unjust to those of us who are supposedly affected by it. The final section takes up the doctrine of primal sin, sin that had its origin prior to the existence of human beings, the theory of sin as uncleanness, and the doctrine of total depravity.

ORIGINAL SIN

The doctrine of original sin states that all human beings have been affected by sins committed by the earliest human beings. It is traditionally understood that these human beings were Adam, the first man, and Eve, the first woman, according to the story of their disobedience in Genesis 3.

This account of original sin is commonly referred to as the Augustinian account of original sin. According to Michael Rea, the doctrine of original sin was accepted by most of the medieval philosopher-theologians from Augustine through Duns Scotus. Moreover, it is affirmed by most of the creeds and confessions (post-Athanasius) of the Orthodox, Roman Catholic, and evangelical Protestant churches. It is not, however, widely held by contemporary thinkers, in part because it appears to conflict with the intuitively plausible principle that person P is morally responsible for a state of affairs S obtaining only if S obtains (or obtained) and P could have prevented S from obtaining (Rea 2007, 319ff).

Although the Augustinian account has not had a great many advocates in the history of philosophy (at least since medieval times), it has had some. Philip Quinn argues that Kant, for example, though he rejects certain aspects of the Augustinian tradition, remains fairly close to it (Quinn 1990, 230).

Five main elements compose the Augustinian doctrine of original sin, according to Jesse Couenhoven. First, original sin has as its source a first sin in the garden of Eden. Second, all of us share in this sin; the reason is that Adam was the progenitor of our race, and we have a solidarity with him. Third, all of us are born with an inherited sin, and this is the result of the first sin. It comes in two forms: common guilt and a constitutional fault (disordered desire and ignorance). Fourth, all human beings are subject to a penalty as the result of inherited sin; the penalty is that our powers are weakened and we die. Fifth, as Augustine speculated, sin and penalty are transmitted from one generation to the next (Couenhoven 2013, 23).

These five elements are not all of equal status. The third is the conceptual heart of the doctrine of original sin. Although these five elements form a more or less affiliated body of subdoctrines, they do not rise or fall together. One could consistently affirm some and reject others.

Michael Rea observes that there are different versions of the doctrine that goes by the name "original sin." One states that all human beings (except for Adam, Eve, Jesus, and possibly his mother) suffer from a kind of corruption that makes it very likely that they will fall into sin. The second asserts that all human beings suffer from a kind of corruption that makes it inevitable that they will fall into sin, and this corruption is a consequence of the first sin of the first man. The third states that all human beings are guilty from birth in the eyes of God, and this guilt is a consequence of the first sin of the first man (Rea 2007, 320).

Eleonore Stump's discussion of original sin begins with three propositions that she describes as Christian beliefs: (1) Adam fell, (2) natural evil (including moral evil) entered the world as a result of Adam's fall, and (3) after death, depending on their state at the time of death, either (a) human beings go to heaven or (b) they go to hell (Stump 1985, 398). Stump believes that these propositions are especially relevant to the problem of evil.

Stump concedes that these propositions will strike many people as implausible or just plain false. But she goes on to argue that although they are controversial and seem false to many people, they are not demonstrably false. To show that this is the case, she provides an interpretation of the doctrine of original sin that is not contradicted by the theory of evolution.

Stump's own interpretation of the doctrine of original sin is summarized by three propositions: (1) At some time in the past, as a result of their own choices, human beings altered their nature for the worse, (2) the alteration involved what we perceive and describe as a change in the nature of human free will, and (3) the changed nature of the will was inheritable (Stump 1985, 402–403). Stump asserts that these propositions are compatible with the denial that there was a particular man, Adam, who made a bad choice and fell from a better to a worse state because the past change in human nature need not have been due to a particular person (they are also compatible with the affirmation that it was Adam who made a bad choice). In addition, Stump contends that the theory of evolution does not entail the falsity of these propositions.

It has often been stated that original sin (although not necessarily the Augustinian version) is the one theological doctrine that is capable of empirical verification. In his book *Shanting Compound* (1966) Langdon Gilkey describes his experiences in a prison camp. He states that the "unpadded" conditions there revealed human nature as it truly is, namely, with a fundamental inclination of the self toward its own welfare. Edward Langerak contends that Gilkey was here influenced by the "realist" theology of Reinhold Niebuhr (Langerak 2014, 22n1). Gilkey sees the behavior of prisoners in a prison camp as empirical verification of the doctrine of original sin.

Michael Ruse (2001) likewise believes that the doctrine is capable of empirical verification. He claims that Darwinian biology empirically supports it. According to him, self-interest runs rapidly into traits such as greed, lust, and boastfulness. There are good biological reasons for this, he says, because original sin is part of the biological package.

In the Orthodox faith the term "original sin" refers to the first sin of Adam and Eve. As a result of this sin, humanity bears the consequences of sin, the chief of which is death. In western traditions, humanity likewise bears the consequences of sin. But the west also understands that humanity is guilty of the sin of Adam and Eve. In the Orthodox Christian understanding, while humanity does bear the consequences of the original sin, humanity does not bear the personal guilt associated with this sin. Adam and Eve were guilty of their willful action; we bear the consequences, chief of which is death. In the Orthodox faith, the term "ancestral sin" is sometimes used to reflect the belief that what is transmitted is not guilt.

The remainder of this section will summarize the account of original sin furnished by the theology of the Roman Catholic Church. Catholic theology envisions original sin as a condition of being deprived of grace. The sin of Adam consists in the lack of sanctifying grace and signifies a turning away from God. Adam was the representative of the whole human race. On his voluntary decision depended either the preservation or the loss of the supernatural endowment, which was a gift to human nature as such. His sin was the sin of the whole human race (Ott 1955, 107ff).

Original sin is transmitted through the natural act of generation. The single sin of Adam is multiplied over and over through natural generation whenever a child of Adam is born.

The soul created by God is good, according to its natural constitution. But God is not obliged to create the soul with the gift of sanctifying grace, and God is not to be blamed for creating new souls without a supernatural endowment. The blame rests with people who misused their freedom. Thus, in the state of original sin a person is deprived of sanctifying grace as well as the gifts of integrity. The lack of the gifts of integrity results in the human race's being subject to concupiscence, suffering, and death. The person stained by original sin is in the imprisonment and slavery of the devil.

This condition should not be thought of as the complete corruption of human nature (in contrast to the view of the reformers). In the condition of original sin God's creatures are able to know religious truths and perform morally good actions. Moreover, free will was not lost because of the sin of Adam.

In baptism original sin is eradicated through the infusion of sanctifying grace. Those who depart this life while still in the state of original sin are excluded from the beatific vision of God.

St. Thomas makes clear that those who depart this life with original sin alone deserve no punishment in addition to this exclusion. If any other punishment were inflicted, a person would be punished out of proportion to his guilt. His guilt did not arise from an action of his own, so he should not be punished by suffering himself. He loses only that which his nature was unable to obtain. In particular, children who die without baptism will not experience sorrow as the result of lacking such a grace (*S.T.*, Appendix, I.Q.1). Catholic theologians usually assume that there is a special place or state for children who die without baptism, which they call *limbus puerorum* (limbo for children), although this is not part of Catholic doctrine.

THE EPISTEMOLOGICAL OR NOETIC EFFECTS OF SIN

Since the seventeenth century it has been widely believed that the doctrine of original sin has epistemological consequences. Pascal held that because all of us suffer from this malady, we wrongly perceived some of the most significant features of reality. Pascal's prescription is natural theology, which he believes can be used to counteract the noetic effects of sin (Cuneo 1994, 646).

Alvin Plantinga makes several claims about the noetic effects of sin. First, sin is in part an affective disorder or malfunction whereby our affections are pointed in the wrong direction. This disorder is presumably (given the context of the discussion) a malfunction of our cognitive faculties. Second, sin affects not only our knowledge of God but also our knowledge of ourselves and other people. Third, sin affects knowledge that is acquired by way of testimony. And, fourth, more indirectly, sin affects our knowledge of the world (A. Plantinga 2000, 206–213).

The examples given by Plantinga involving our knowledge of other people include thinking them inferior and misestimating or misunderstanding their attitudes toward us. For an example of sin affecting knowledge acquired by testimony, consider this: Suppose a sinful attitude on my part causes me to regard an acquaintance of mine as a liar. As a result, I might attach much less credulity to his testimony than I would if I lacked this sinful attitude. This attitude would then qualify as a noetic effect of sin because my presumption of his habitual lying would affect how I regarded his testimony.

An example of sin affecting my knowledge of the world might be the following: A sinful attitude on my part might cause me to doubt many of the pronouncements of the scientific community, and as a result I might develop a distorted view of nature. I might judge that science is mistaken when it claims that the vaccinations that are routinely given to children do not cause autism. Or I might judge that science is mistaken when it claims that manmade global warming is taking place.

Finally, as noted in the previous section, Couenhoven believes that Augustinian original sin can result in ignorance. By this I take him to mean that sin blinds us from the knowledge of certain truths about reality.

THE ALLEGED UNFAIRNESS OF THE DOCTRINE

People commonly allege that the doctrine of original sin is unfair: Since we are living thousands of years after Adam and Eve sinned, we are in no way morally responsible for what they did. How, then, can it be fair that we in some manner are affected by or held to account for what they did?

There are several questions of unfairness that one might raise regarding original sin. Leibniz poses one in *Confessio Philosophi*: Couldn't God have replaced Adam and Eve after their fall with better creatures, and wouldn't this have prevented their sins from being transmitted to future generations? Leibniz (1699) answers this question by essentially saying that if God had followed that course of action, a very different series of circumstances would have occurred, including different marriages, and very different people would have been born. Therefore, we have no reason to be angry at God for allowing them to sin; our very existence depends on the toleration of their sins. Had they not been tolerated, people different from ourselves would have existed instead.

Robert Merrihew Adams believes that Leibniz's response to the unfairness question is correct (Adams 1987, 66). A person could easily have existed without some of the evils of the actual world (for example, future evils). But past evils that have profoundly affected the course of human history are different. Adams notes that his parents probably would not have met or married had it not been for World War I, and as a result he would not have been born.

We might object that Leibniz has not solved the central unfairness issue. Recall Rea's observation from section one that the doctrine of original sin appears to conflict with the intuitively plausible principle that person *P* is morally responsible for obtaining a state of affairs *S* only if *S* obtains (or obtained) and *P* could have prevented *S* from obtaining. The conflict Rea seems to have in mind is this: According to the Augustinian account of original sin, all of us have been affected by the sins of Adam and Eve and are hence morally responsible for obtaining the state of affairs of their sinning. But none of us has the ability to prevent this state of affairs from obtaining; hence, according to the principle cited by Rea, none of us is morally responsible for its obtaining. From this one might well conclude that it is unfair to hold us responsible for the sinful acts of Adam and Eve, so the doctrine of original sin should be rejected.

In response, an advocate for the doctrine might defend a version of it different than what has traditionally been understood as the Augustinian account. Sometimes the sin that affects all members of the human race is described in terms of taint: Though we are not culpable, we are nevertheless tainted by the sins of Adam and Eve. According to this way of thinking, human beings can be tainted by the evil acts of others to whom they are connected in some significant manner. Although they are not culpable of these actions or their outcomes, their moral integrity is nevertheless affected (Appiah 1991, 229). Another way to describe what is essentially the same phenomenon is in terms of defilement, a symbolic stain (Ricoeur 1967, 35–37). According to this way of thinking, if we have been defiled by the sins of our original ancestors, the defilement takes the form of a symbolic stain. Although the doctrine of original sin has been controversial for centuries, perhaps analyzing it in terms of taint or stain rather than culpability confers some plausibility on it. (Appiah's views will be discussed in more detail in chapter 3.)

Consider once again the principle cited by Rea, the principle that a person is morally responsible for a state of affairs obtaining only if the person could have prevented it from happening. This principle no longer conflicts with the doctrine of original sin when it is understood in terms of moral taint. A proponent of this version of the doctrine can be happy to acknowledge that we are not morally responsible for the sinful behavior of Adam and Eve. We are merely tainted by their sinful behavior. The responsibility part of the doctrine no longer applies.

PRIMAL SIN, SIN AS UNCLEANNESS, AND TOTAL DEPRAVITY

This section contains additional views about sin that fall under the rubric of sin understood as a fundamental feature of the human condition.

Primal Sin

In addition to original sin there is a phenomenon called primal sin, the sin of the angels who freely rebelled against God. Augustine regards the stories of creaturely falls in scripture to consist of free choices that have resulted in the origins of evil. The sins of Adam and Eve in the garden gave rise to original sin, while evil free choices on the part of angels account for primal sin. Primal sin preceded the sins of Adam and Eve. Augustine regarded the serpent in the story of Adam and Eve's fall as having been used by the devil and regarded the devil as a fallen angel.

Scott MacDonald points out that the sins of the angels deserve to be called primal not just because they preceded the sins of human beings but also because they constituted something new in creation (MacDonald 1999, 110). The first evil, says MacDonald, appears against a backdrop of total goodness. Everything created by God is wholly good and without defect, and this includes the creatures with rationality who freely choose evil.

Sin as Uncleanness

Marilyn McCord Adams argues that sin, at its most basic level, is uncleanness. As such, it is an outgrowth of two metaphysical roots (Adams 1999, 94).

The first metaphysical root is the metaphysical gap. The so-called size gap between ourselves and God misfits us for each other's company. Humans are flimsy, temporary, and vulnerable to attack from all sorts of things, and nothing we could naturally be or do would make us suitable for God's company. Because God and creatures are so radically different in kind, it is difficult to see how God and humans could ever occupy the same social world.

The second metaphysical root is metaphysical straddling. Human nature seems unclean in itself because it is not simply one kind or another. The heterogeneity of human nature is sometimes conceptualized as soul and body, spirit and matter, or personal and animal. Traditional anthropologies see the material, corporeal, and animal distracting the mind's cognitive and evaluative attention and luring it into preferring lesser goods to greater. At the same time, mind interferes with matter, trying to impose its own agenda. The human straddles the spiritual and the material and thus is neither one kind nor the other.

Total Depravity

The Augustinian doctrine of original sin has led many to embrace a doctrine known as total depravity. The doctrine of total depravity states that human beings are so corrupt that they are unable to do any good and are inclined toward all evil. Many adherents of this doctrine go on to believe that if and only if human beings are born again are they capable of rising out of this dire condition. But left to their own devices, human beings are helpless to escape this condition of all-encompassing sin and depravity.

The doctrine of original sin does not entail the doctrine of total depravity. After all, being tainted by Adam's sin doesn't entail that one is totally incapable of good works. But two Reformed confessional statements of the sixteenth century, the 1562 Belgic Confession and the 1563

Heidelberg Catechism, link them together in such a way as to suggest that the one follows quite naturally from the other.

Finally, related to total depravity is the notion of transworld depravity, which was introduced by Alvin Plantinga in his account of the free will defense. Plantinga's definition of transworld depravity is quite lengthy and complex, but the basic idea, according to Paul Tidman, is this: "Moral agents suffer from transworld deparavity if they are such that if they were created they would go wrong with respect to at least one moral choice. The core of the Free Will Defense is the claim that it is possible that no matter who God created it was true that they would have performed at least some wrong actions" (Tidman 2008, 400). Suppose that a possible creature (one that exists in at least some possible world) is such that if he were to exist in the actual world he would sin at least once. Then, according to Tidman's formulation of Plantinga's definition, this possible creature would suffer from transworld depravity. The notion of transworld depravity will be discussed in greater detail in chapter 9.

CHAPTER TWO

INDIVIDUAL AND COLLECTIVE SINS

When sin is approached in the moral realm as a property borne by actions, many possibilities are open to one. The first section of this chapter examines four such possibilities, together with a brief discussion of the concept of atonement. The second section defends the position that the claim that sins have been committed by a group or collective makes sense in certain contexts. This section also discusses ascriptions of guilt to groups or collectives (popularly known as collective guilt) for having committed sins of this type.

SINFUL ACTIONS, ATONEMENT, AND SCAPEGOATS

How are sinful actions to be characterized or identified? In this section I will begin by describing four possibilities. First, a sinful action can be envisioned as one that violates a moral duty or obligation (or one that consists in the failure to satisfy a duty or obligation). Second, a sinful act can be identified as one that is worthy of moral blame. Third, a sinful act can be classified as an act to which moral guilt is an appropriate response. Fourth, one can stipulate that any act that is offensive or displeasing to a particular deity counts as a sinful act. No doubt other possibilities present themselves, but for our present purposes these will suffice.

The first approach has much to recommend it. One can agree that the violation of a moral obligation is a relatively serious matter. Regardless of how one accounts for the basis or origin of a moral obligation, it is not only wrong to violate a moral obligation; it is also forbidden. To the extent that one regards sin as something morally wrong or forbidden, one might find it appealing to hold that one commits a sinful act whenever one violates a moral obligation.

The second approach identifies a sinful act as one that is worthy of moral blame. To commit an act that is morally blameworthy, according to this approach, is to commit a sinful act. According to this way of thinking, sin consists of any action, omission, or state that is inherently blameworthy (Adams 1985, 3n2). If one agrees with the claim that it is always morally blameworthy to violate a moral obligation, as seems reasonable, the first approach turns out to be a special case of the second approach. The second approach acknowledges sins that are morally blameworthy but fall short of qualifying as morally forbidden (where a forbidden act is one that violates a moral obligation).

Acts that are morally blameworthy but not morally forbidden are called "offences." One example is that of lingering at one's table in a restaurant when others are known to be waiting for tables (Chisholm and Sosa 1966, 326). Other things being equal, a sin that consists in the violation of a moral obligation is more blameworthy than a sin that consists of an offence. Thus, sins that are only slightly blameworthy count as sins in spite of their not violating moral obligations. Some might be tempted to suppose that any act that qualifies as morally blameworthy also qualifies as morally forbidden (and that approach one and approach two turn out to be equivalent). But the problem with this view is that sins that are only slightly blameworthy are then classified as forbidden, and it is not clear how they differ from seriously blameworthy sins that violate moral obligations (more will be said about the variability of sins in terms of seriousness in chapter 4). It seems preferable to maintain a separation between sins of offence and sins that involve violating moral obligations.

The third approach identifies sin as something for which moral guilt is appropriate. Just as someone who breaks the law is guilty of a crime, someone who breaks the moral law is guilty of having done so and can be said to have committed a sin. According to this view, sins are analogous to crimes; sins are to the moral law what crimes are to the law of the land.

Augustine describes in his *Confessions* (ed. Oates, 1948) the feelings of guilt he experienced when committing sins in his earlier life. These passages demonstrate an understanding of responsibility for sins and a sense that feelings of guilt are an appropriate response to sins. Thomas Aquinas believed that a person who chooses to act in a sinful manner incurs guilt. For him, sin is a violation of both the divine and natural law, and the greater a person's will to sin, the greater the guilt he or she incurs.

The fourth approach envisions sin as that which is offensive or displeasing to a particular deity. Cornelius Plantinga characterizes sin as any act—any thought, desire, emotion, word, or deed—or its particular absence that displeases God and deserves blame. He goes on to say that the disposition to sin also displeases God, and hence "sin" refers to both act and disposition. Thus, all sin has first and foremost a Godward force (C. Plantinga 1995, 13).

According to Plantinga, God hates sin not just because it violates his law but because it violates shalom. It interferes with the way things are supposed to be. Sin, he says, is culpable shalom-breaking. It disrupts something good and harmonious; it is like an intruder. Shalom is God's design for creation and redemption, and sin is human vandalism of these. Consequently, sin is an affront to their architect and builder (ibid.).

Richard Swinburne asserts that man's dependence on God is so total that he owes it to God to live a good life. Failure to do this counts as sin. If a man fails in a duty to others, he fails in his duty toward God. Swinburne distinguishes between sinning objectively and sinning subjectively. A man sins objectively if he does what is wrong, and this is true whether or not he realizes that what he does is wrong. If a man does what he believes to be wrong, he sins subjectively because he is acting against his conception of the good (Swinburne 1989, 124).

Swinburne believes that a man can sin subjectively even if he does not believe that he wrongs God, for he might not acknowledge God's existence. But if he sins in the belief that he wrongs God, that is a greater sin than if he sins without the belief that he wrongs God.

An important distinction to be recognized by those who take this approach is that between being and act. If sin is a turning from God, it must be located in whatever is deemed to be the center of selfhood and considered a continuing state of being rather than a momentary act. As a state of being, sin affects the entire person from whom specific acts arise.

Thus it is appropriate to confess our sin, which endures as a state of mind and heart, as well as to confess specific acts or sins.

Clearly, these four approaches are not mutually exclusive. One can consistently affirm more than one of these approaches. As noted above, approach one appears to be a special case of approach two for the simple reason that it is always morally blameworthy to violate one's moral obligation. Thus one can assent to both approach one and approach two.

Likewise, one can assent to both approaches three and four. One can hold that moral guilt is an appropriate response to sin and that sin can be identified as that which is offensive or displeasing to a particular god. One could simply affirm that guilt is an appropriate response to sin *because* it is offensive to a deity.

Perhaps these four approaches can be thought of as different emphases in characterizing sin. Approach two, for example, emphasizes the fact that sins can be trifling, since even mildly blameworthy acts can count as sins. Approach four emphasizes the idea that sins cannot exist apart from some type of deity. And approach three emphasizes the responses human beings should take toward their sins.

Several of the world religions have articulated in one form or another a doctrine of atonement, a doctrine that stipulates that the sins one has committed can be forgiven, wiped away, or transferred somewhere else. Naturally, it is beyond the scope of this book to catalog and discuss the doctrines of atonement adopted by various world religions. Instead, I will focus on one of the oldest formulations of the doctrine, the formulation adopted by the Jewish tradition. According to this tradition, the sins of an entire group of people can be transferred to a scapegoat.

In the book of Leviticus chapter 16 the ceremony performed on the Day of Atonement is described. The priest lays a hand on the head of a goat, and the goat is subsequently driven into the desert. The goat experiences suffering not on account of its own blemish or defect but on account of the sins that have been laid upon it. This is the context for understanding the New Testament's language of sacrifice. If we understand sacrifice in this manner, we have a doctrine of penal substitution (Hare 1996, 257).

The goat is described in verse 10 as a scapegoat. The sins of the people have been laid upon the goat, and they are removed from the people and sent into the wilderness. This ritual constitutes one understanding of what the sacrifice of Christ means in the context of the Hebrew sacrificial cult (ibid.).

Modern usage of the term "scapegoat" does not presuppose that a transference of sin or guilt is thought to take place. Nor does modern usage imply or connote the complete lack of defect characteristic of the goat (a fact that allowed the Christian tradition to draw a parallel between the goat and Jesus). But it does retain the idea that someone is chosen, frequently with some degree of arbitrariness, as the sole or primary bearer of guilt or blame for something that has happened. And it seems to retain in addition the idea that some sort of transference takes place, a transference that is not one of sin or guilt.

The scapegoat, according to modern usage, is blamed for something that happens out of proportion to what he or she deserves. The scapegoat is not, generally speaking, entirely innocent of contributing to the unwanted state of affairs, but a sin greater than what was actually committed is attributed to the scapegoat by those who make him or her a scapegoat (Andrade 2014).

The transference that takes place is one of shame. By virtue of being a scapegoat, one is shamed as a result of being blamed to an exaggerated degree for one's role. This does not imply that the scapegoat becomes more shameful, for the transference of shame is undeserved. In the eyes of others, the scapegoat appears more shameful, but the scapegoat is not in reality more shameful.

Because modern usage of the term "scapegoat" does not imply a complete lack of sin or defect with respect to the unwanted state of affairs, a different term is used to apply to situations in which someone completely innocent is blamed for what happens. That term is "sacrificial lamb." When someone is made a sacrificial lamb, he or she is presumed to bear no blame whatsoever for the unwanted state of affairs. More will be said about the moral status of scapegoats in chapter 8.

COLLECTIVE SINS AND COLLECTIVE GUILT

In the first part of this section I will discuss the view that sins can be committed by groups or collectives of moral agents. I will show that in some instances sense can be made of the assertion that a sin has been committed by a collective, while in other instances such a claim is highly misleading. In the second part of the section I will address the topic of collective guilt.

Not only are the actions of individual moral agents often described as sinful, but the same is also sometimes claimed of the actions of groups of moral agents. It is commonly claimed that various individuals working toward a common purpose have sinned in their joint endeavors. These joint endeavors might range from an assassination plot to a robbery involving several participants to something as benign as a plot to deceive a co-worker into thinking that her car has been stolen from the office parking lot. In each of these cases one might claim that the group in question has performed sinful actions.

One might object that only the actions of individual moral agents can attain the status of being sinful and that being sinful is not a property of group actions. This objection might be based on a conviction that there are no such things as group actions, but it might also be based on a conviction that the property of being sinful cannot correctly be predicated of group actions.

I believe that this objection can be better understood by making reference to the debate between those who believe collective responsibility is possible and those who disagree. For if it is possible for a collective consisting of several individuals to be morally responsible for a harmful state of affairs as the result of their individual sinful contributions to it, the door has been opened to the possibility of ascribing sinfulness to a collective.

Collective responsibility can be characterized as the view that a collective consisting of two or more agents can bear moral responsibility for a state of affairs. One who opposes the possibility of collective responsibility might object to ascribing moral responsibility to a collective that, in and of itself, is an abstract object. But one might also object on the grounds that individuals are the only bearers of moral responsibility and that it is unfair to hold someone responsible for something that is due, in whole or in part, to the actions of others. According to this view, one can have moral responsibility only for one's own actions or omissions, regardless of whether the resulting state of affairs can also be attributed to the actions of other agents. Proponents of this view include H. D. Lewis, Steven Sverdlik, Martin Benjamin, Suemas Miller, Jan Narveson, and many others.

Those who have argued in favor of the possibility of collective responsibility assert that not all instances of collective responsibility can be neatly reduced to ascriptions of responsibility to individual moral agents. People must sometimes be held accountable for harmful outcomes that go beyond what can be identified as the result of certain individuals performing particular actions. Proponents of this view include Larry May, Peter French, Virginia Held, D. E. Cooper, and many others.

Those arguing for an individualist approach sometimes concede (as does Sverdlik) that several moral agents can bear moral responsibility for the same state of affairs, a situation in which they can be said to share moral responsibility (although Lewis denies that this is possible). But what they deny is that a collective can bear moral responsibility for an outcome when some members of the collective fail to bear responsibility *as individuals* for the same outcome. And what they deny even more vigorously is that a collective can bear moral responsibility for an outcome when *none* of the members bear responsibility as individuals for the same outcome. Even those who argue in favor of the possibility of collective responsibility frequently exhibit a reluctance to acknowledge the possibility of this latter situation.

Given this backdrop, let us return to the question of whether being sinful is a property that can properly be ascribed to groups or collectives. Suppose that four teenage boys push someone's car into a lake, and suppose that the action of each teenager qualifies as a sin. Would it be natural to assert that what the group or collective of teenagers did was sinful? I believe it would. In this situation, it would seem perfectly reasonable to describe pushing the car into the lake as sinful.

Consider next a situation in which three of the teenagers push the car into the lake while the fourth stands by and offers words of encouragement. On the assumption that the actions of all four teenagers qualify as sins, does it make sense to assert that what the group did was sinful? I believe that it does, but the situation is more ambiguous than previously. One might argue that the sin committed by the fourth boy differs from the sins of the first three, and hence it is misleading to say that what the group did was sinful.

If this seems a bit of an over-reaction, imagine that in addition to the four teenagers mentioned there is a fifth teenager, a security guard whose job it is to keep an eye on the cars parked in the vicinity of the lake. He recognizes the car being pushed as belonging to a particularly arrogant and obnoxious individual and takes great delight in remaining silent as the deed is carried out. Surely we can agree that under the circumstances his omitting to say or do anything to prevent the car from being pushed into the lake is sinful. But to assert that what the five teenagers did is sinful is misleading at best. Assertions of this type can easily lead one to become skeptical of the view that sinfulness can properly be ascribed to groups or collectives.

Recall those who argue against the possibility of collective responsibility on the grounds that it is unfair to hold someone responsible for something that is due, in whole or in part, to the actions of others. Someone of this persuasion would deny that the five teenagers are collectively responsible for the car's being pushed into the lake. Rather, each is responsible for his individual contribution, whether it be pushing, encouraging, or failing to say or do anything to prevent the outcome.

In like manner, one might argue that the assertion that what the five teenagers did was sinful is highly misleading. Each boy committed a sin in connection with the car's ending up in the lake, and each contributed to the car's ending up in the lake. But the sins of the fourth and fifth teenagers differ significantly from the sins of the first three. The assertion that what the five teenagers did was sinful encourages the misconception that they acted similarly, while the fifth teenager is guilty of an intentional omission.

Perhaps the correct conclusion to draw from this discussion is that it makes sense to acknowledge the possibility of group or collective sins in situations in which the individual sinful actions are relevantly similar, but not otherwise. What counts as relevantly similar? We could stipulate that a sinful omission is not relevantly similar to an action that is sinful. We could stipulate that relevantly similar sinful actions are actions committed with a common goal in mind. We could stipulate that, whenever the actions of several persons constitute a group action, the door is opened to the possibility that their individual sins are constituents of a collective sin.

To further understand responsibility in contexts involving multiple participants, let us now turn to the topic of collective guilt. Earlier in this chapter the view that a sinful act can be classified as an act for which guilt is an appropriate response was mentioned as a possibility for characterizing sinful acts. But not only are individual moral agents said to experience guilt for their sinful actions; groups or collectives are also commonly said to experience guilt (and here it is important to distinguish between feelings of guilt and actual guilt on the part of the members of the groups or collectives).

Perhaps the classic example of collective guilt in the philosophical literature is the guilt experienced by the German people following the Second World War regarding the events of the Holocaust. The collective guilt experienced by the German people has been widely discussed. Commentators have sometimes remarked that these feelings of guilt have been misplaced because the vast majority of the population had nothing to do with the events of the Holocaust; in other words, the vast majority of them committed no sinful actions connected to the events of the Holocaust.

In his book *Sharing Responsibility* (1992), May argues that twentieth-century existentialist thought can shed much light on questions connected with moral responsibility. The concept of moral responsibility in twentieth-century existentialist thought was shaped largely by the writings of philosophers such as Jean-Paul Sartre, Karl Jaspers, and Hannah Arendt. Writing in the years after the Second World War, they tried to come to terms with the widespread failure of their fellow citizens to prevent the horrible actions of the Nazis. May observes that they turned to existentialist thought in an effort to explain this profound failure, and they appealed to the resources of existentialist thought to design an adequate theory of responsibility. An adequate theory, they believed, is characterized by its ability to take seriously society and the problems that afflict it.

Having been inspired by this tradition, May develops an existentialist approach to questions of group or collective responsibility. His approach is built on the idea that groups have a powerful influence over their members, in particular on their attitudes and behavior. As the result of belonging to a group, an individual's personal values undergo a transformation. People belonging to groups discover that the various members influence and transform the values of one another. And along with this sharing of attitudes and values comes a sharing of responsibility for group actions. May contends that belonging to groups also tends to make people insensitive to various harms in such a way that they come to share responsibility for these harms.

Sometimes groups are responsible for inaction. May describes situations in which members decide not to act as collective omissions. Moreover, there are cases in which people with the ability to form a group to prevent harm from occurring fail to act. May refers to this type of situation as collective inaction. These putative groups can often be judged collectively responsible for their inaction or even for the harms they fail to prevent. Their members are not necessarily guilty of their inaction or of these harms; it is more appropriate for them to feel shame for their inaction or collective guilt for these harms. May emphasizes that there is a potential for great social good when people seek solutions of a social nature; the reason is that groups are far more likely than individuals to be able to prevent significant harms from occurring.

May's discussion is intended to push to the limit how we ought to think about agency and responsibility. People who are products of western culture are inclined to think of responsibility as set at a rather modest level, and May challenges these ways of thinking. He quotes Hannah Arendt as saying, "This taking upon ourselves the consequences for things we are entirely innocent of, is the price we pay for the fact that we live our lives not by ourselves but . . . [within] a human community" (May 1992, xi). This statement provides a basis for understanding why the German people feel shame and a sense of collective guilt for the actions of Nazi officials. Because we live in a human community, Arendt believes that there is a sense in which we take upon ourselves the consequences of the harmful acts of others.

The sinful actions of others produce harmful states of affairs in the human community, but because we live within this community, according to Arendt, there is a sense in which we take these consequences upon ourselves. Although the German people were entirely innocent of the sinful actions of the Nazi officials, existentialists such as Arendt can help us understand why they experience collective guilt. I will revisit the topic of collective guilt in chapter 8.

CHAPTER THREE

ACCESSORY SINS

Medieval authors engaged in a great deal of discussion regarding accessory sins, sins that are committed when one contributes to the wrongdoing of another. In his book *The Treatise on Vices and Virtues in Latin and the Vernacular*, historian Richard Newhauser identifies a total of nine accessory sins. The first five fall under the category of people who are in positions of authority and misuse their own power. They do so (1) by commanding, (2) by protecting, (3) by making use of, (4) by concealing, and (5) by not opposing the actual commission of sin by another. The remaining four accessory sins fall under the category of people who support someone to whom one is subordinate in the misuse of power. They do so (1) by giving advice, (2) by agreeing with, (3) by praising, and (4) by not revealing the commission of a sin (Newhauser 1993, 194).

In this chapter I will suggest that the accessory sins of the medieval philosophers fall under the rubric of what modern thinkers describe as acts of complicit wrongdoing. I take as a point of departure the nine accessory sins of Thomas Aquinas (*S.T.*, Pt. II-II, Q. 62, 7). After offering a characterization of complicity, I will discuss the scheme of Aquinas in a fair amount of depth. Then I will turn to the modern notion of complicity and illustrate how, understood in terms of one's performing sinful actions that contribute to the harms caused by the sinful actions of another, it is possible to avoid being complicit. In the final section I will take up the topic of moral luck and describe its relevance to avoiding becoming complicit in the sinful actions of another.

ACCESSORY SINS IN AQUINAS

Suppose that an agent performs a wrongful act in order to bring about an outcome the agent desires. A person is complicit in the agent's performance of the act if the person performs an act (which might be an intentional omission) in an effort to contribute to the outcome in the sense of making it more likely to occur. In every instance of complicity there is a principal actor, and in some cases there are more than one principal actors. In every instance of complicity, the principal actor performs an action (or omits performing an action) that produces an outcome. For the purposes of this discussion, I will assume that this outcome is in some sense harmful, or at least unwanted by society.

The accomplices are moral agents that perform actions that contribute to this outcome. Throughout this discussion I will refer to these actions as "contributing actions" with the understanding that they might take the form of omissions. Here it is essential to note that the accomplices are contributing to the outcome. They are not contributing to the relevant actions of the principal actor; indeed, in many cases an accomplice's contributing actions are taken after the principal actor has performed his or her action. It is also essential to note that the contributing action of an accomplice need not causally contribute to the outcome; in cases in which an accomplice's contributing action consists of an omission, it will fall short of constituting a causal contribution.

Typically the principal actor initiates a chain of events producing an outcome, and one or more accomplices perform actions contributing to the outcome. But occasionally an accomplice initiates a chain of events leading to the production of an outcome by a principal actor. This can happen when someone commands a second person to produce a harmful outcome, and that person subsequently does so. The person who produces the outcome as the result of being commanded to do so is the principal actor, and the person who commanded him or her to do so is an accomplice. Normally a principal actor bears more moral blame for the outcome than an accomplice, but in a situation in which an accomplice commands the principal actor to produce a harmful outcome, it might well be that the accomplice bears more blame for the outcome than the principal actor.

The nine accessory sins identified by Thomas Aquinas are the following. Someone can be an accomplice by way of (1) commanding another to do something, (2) counseling someone about how to do something, (3) consenting or offering permission to undertake a course of action, (4) offering flattery or encouragement to another, (5) "receiving" or covering for another after the fact, (6) participating in a project of another, (7) remaining silent about the wrongdoing of another, (8) failing to prevent the wrongdoing of another, and (9) failing to denounce the wrongdoing of another.

Several words of explanation are in order. First, the ninth way of being an accomplice is a special case of the seventh. The failure to denounce wrongdoing is one manner in which a person can remain silent about the wrongdoing of another. Second, Aquinas attaches a condition to the eighth and ninth ways of being complicit, and that is the condition that one must be bound or obligated to prevent or denounce the wrongdoing. If I confront a person about to commit a wrongdoing, and then, if I fail to prevent or denounce, I am an accomplice only if I have a moral obligation to prevent or denounce. This seems to be a reasonable stipulation. If I stand by and watch a child point a firearm at a younger child, I am an accomplice for failing to prevent the subsequent shooting. But if I stand by and do nothing while a terrorist fires shots at people in a public place, then, depending upon the details of the situation, I am not an accomplice. This is because I presumably have a moral obligation to act in the example of the child with a firearm, and I do not have a moral obligation (because it is too dangerous) to attempt to disarm the terrorist.

Before moving on, a disclaimer is necessary. Aquinas does not actually refer to these nine ways of being an accomplice as forms of complicity. Rather, in the passage from which these nine ways are extracted he is discussing the conditions under which people are bound to make restitution for property that has been taken from someone else. Clearly people are obligated to make restitution of property taken from someone else. But the main point of Aquinas's discussion is that someone can be obligated to make restitution of the property of another when someone other than oneself actually seizes the property. The nine ways comprise the ways in which this phenomenon can occur. Aquinas is speaking about complicity in theft, but he does not actually describe it as complicity.

When one contemplates the taxonomy of Aquinas, it becomes evident that the nine ways of becoming complicit are not equally serious from a moral perspective. The most serious might be commanding another to commit a wrongdoing and participating in a wrongful scheme initiated by another. These modes of behavior almost certainly cause an accomplice to bear moral responsibility for the outcome, and normally in these situations the principal actor and the accomplice are both morally responsible for the outcome (though they need not be equally responsible for it).

Of the other ways of being complicit, counseling someone to do wrong and consenting to the wrongdoing of another place one within the boundaries of qualifying as morally responsible for the outcome in question. This is partly due to the fact that complicit moral agents are enabling harm or at least facilitating harm. Normally a person bears moral responsibility for the harm produced by a principal actor's wrongful behavior when the person has counseled him or her to engage in this behavior or consented to his or her engaging in this behavior (assuming consent is something the principal actor believes necessary).

The other five ways of becoming complicit in the scheme of Aquinas involve less active roles for the complicit agents, and for this reason there tends to be less likelihood of this agent's incurring moral responsibility for the outcome in question. Flattery (encouraging) and receiving (covering for) require action on the part of the accomplice, but except for extreme cases, such as providing refuge for an escaped convict, these activities are ordinarily sufficiently benign that one does not incur moral responsibility for the outcome (but of course, one nevertheless incurs moral responsibility for one's actions of encouragement or covering for someone else).

The three remaining ways of becoming complicit—silence, failure to prevent, and failure to denounce—require little or no action on the part of the accomplice. In certain cases, failures such as these can cause one to become morally responsible for the outcome in question. If a nurse observes another nurse administering the wrong medication to a patient and does nothing, the observing nurse presumably bears responsibility for the resulting harm to the patient (recall that Aquinas stipulates that the failure to prevent qualifies as complicity when one has a moral obligation to prevent what happens). In typical situations, however, complicity that takes the form of failing to act does not involve one's bearing moral responsibility for the outcome, even when the omission is intentional. If I observe a total stranger parking in a no parking zone and say nothing, that does not make me responsible for the presence of her automobile in that location.

In the remainder of this section it will be my contention that, when the accomplice fails to bear responsibility for such an outcome, the accomplice can still be tainted by the wrongful actions of the principal actor.

The basic idea is that a moral agent who commits a wrongdoing sometimes taints those to whom he or she is closely connected. An entire family, for example, can be tainted by the criminal actions of a son or daughter. Not only are their reputations damaged, but on a deeper level their moral integrity is affected.

Anthony Appiah, the first to introduce the notion of tainting into the philosophical literature (1991), believes that moral taint is produced when the wrongful actions of another produce harm and the contagion of this wrongdoing is transferred to someone with no involvement. Consider once again the events of the Holocaust. Ordinary German citizens bore no responsibility for these events, but Appiah believes they were nevertheless tainted by the actions of Nazi officials. This means that they experienced a loss of moral integrity. Someone's own moral integrity, according to Appiah, is affected when someone else produces harm and there is some connection between these two persons. Moral taint is a phenomenon that involves one's links to others in the community.

Appiah's primary example of moral taint is holding shares of stock in firms doing business in South Africa in the 1980s. Someone holding shares in these companies bore no responsibility for the harm produced by apartheid, but he or she was nevertheless tainted by the persons who practiced apartheid. Those purchasing shares in these companies experienced a diminishing of moral integrity, and, according to Appiah, it was appropriate for them to experience shame. Those who are tainted by the actions of others need not feel guilt. Feeling guilt is not appropriate for an individual who has no personal involvement in what happens or for one who incurs no moral responsibility for the outcome.

It might be objected that the notion of moral taint is flimsy, that it is hard to see how it impugns one's integrity, and that there is no reason to care if one is tainted by the misdeeds of another. I believe Appiah would be happy to concede that it is flimsy, at least compared to the notion of moral responsibility, and that it impugns one's integrity to a degree that is perhaps vanishingly small. But from this it does not follow that there is no reason to care whether one is tainted. Suppose that in the 1980s I was shocked to learn that I was a stockholder in a company that did business in South Africa, and I immediately sold the stock because I was conscientious about doing the right thing. Thus, I had a reason to care about the fact that I was tainted because I believed that my own integrity was somewhat impugned. Even if Appiah is mistaken in thinking that one's integrity is affected whenever one is tainted, one can still have a good reason to care.

I suggest that moral taint can shed light on situations in which an accomplice falls short of bearing moral responsibility for the harm produced by the principal actor. When the complicity of a moral agent takes the form of commanding, counseling, consenting, and participating, he or she normally bears responsibility for the resulting harm. But when the complicity takes one of the other five forms, a person's contribution to the sequence of events might be limited enough that he or she falls short of bearing responsibility for the outcome. On occasions when this happens, one may be tempted to suppose that one has done nothing wrong and that nothing has happened to affect one's moral integrity. But one of the lessons to be learned from Appiah's account of moral taint is that an accomplice can be tainted by the wrongful actions of a principal actor, and the moral integrity of the accomplice can as a result be affected. To prevent being tainted in situations such as these, one can attempt to distance oneself from the principal actor and his or her wrongful actions. Appiah's discussion of moral taint will be re-visited in chapter 8.

AVOIDING ACCESSORY SINS

In this section I will assume that the medieval philosophers are correct in classifying actions of complicity in wrongdoing as sins. This is an assumption tied closely to the idea that being complicit in the wrongful actions of a principal actor is always morally blameworthy. I will assume in addition that a moral agent should in general avoid performing sinful acts.

These assumptions taken together lead us to the following question: How can moral agents avoid committing accessory sins?

Suppose that a principal actor performs a sinful action in the hope of producing a particular outcome, and someone is in a position to become an accomplice by contributing to the outcome. How can this person avoid becoming an accomplice? The obvious answer is not to perform a contributing act. But a more interesting and illuminating answer is at the same time an answer to the question how to interfere with the outcome, and that is to take steps to prevent the outcome from occurring. In the spirit of Aquinas's enumeration of nine accessory sins, I shall list ways that correspond to each of the nine.

First, a person can command someone else to cease from committing sinful actions, as when a mother shopping with her son in a store commands him to put back an item she knows he was planning to shoplift. Second, a person can counsel another to refrain from sinful behavior by explaining that the behavior will lead to unforeseen consequences. Third, a person can consent to someone's not performing a sinful action. For instance, suppose that an employer ordered an employee to perform an action that was morally wrong, then changed his mind and gave the employee permission to refrain from the action.

Fourth, someone can participate in sinful activity with the intent of sabotaging it, as when an undercover police officer participates in criminal activity only because she intends to arrest the other participants. Fifth, an individual can use flattery to encourage someone to refrain from sinful activity. A college student knows that her boyfriend is tempted to cheat on a homework assignment; she then tells him that he is highly intelligent and has no need to cheat. Suitably flattered, he does not do so. Sixth, a person can cover for another in such a way as to frustrate the sinful plans of the other. Suppose that one of my friends is a suspect in a crime that I know he committed. I provide an alibi for my friend so contrived and outlandish as to render him the prime suspect.

Seventh, one can avoid becoming complicit by not denouncing the sins of another. On a street corner a disabled man is being harassed by a total stranger. Someone else comes to the rescue of the disabled man by assaulting the stranger. A merchant looking out at the scene is in a position to denounce the assaulter but decides not to, thereby guaranteeing that he is not complicit in the harassment of the disabled person. Eighth, one can interfere in the sinful actions of another by way of silence. A friend of mine is caught stealing merchandise from the store that I own. When he is caught by police, he falsely claims that I gave him permission. However, when asked if I gave him permission, I simply remain silent. My silence is intended to convey the message that he is lying, and as a result he is arrested. Ninth, one can interfere in the sinful actions of another by not preventing a situation from taking place. One day I see a friend about to sell an illegal weapon to someone that I recognize as an assistant prosecutor. I decide not to step in to prevent him from doing so, and as a result his career of selling illegal weapons is put decisively to an end.

SIN AND MORAL LUCK

Having seen in the previous section that one can take steps to ensure that one is not complicit in an outcome brought about by the sinful actions of another, it remains to be seen how one can avoid becoming complicit in such an outcome without taking any action whatsoever. In this section it will be my suggestion that moral luck can play a role in sparing one from becoming an accomplice in someone else's sinful activity, although I should confess at the outset that not everyone shares my conviction that moral luck is possible (more on this follows).

For those unfamiliar with the concept of moral luck, Judith Jarvis Thomson (1989) offers the following example. Bert, a habitually careful driver, almost always backs out of his driveway after first looking. One day he fails to look before backing out because something he hears on the radio distracts him. Tragically, he strikes a child who happens to be darting across his driveway, and the child dies. Carol also habitually looks first before backing out of her driveway, but she fails to look on the same day that Bert fails to look. Fortunately, no one happens to be crossing her driveway at that moment.

No one would dispute the claim that Carol is lucky that her failure had no unfortunate consequences. But does her luck rise to the level of moral luck? If one answers this question in the affirmative, one is agreeing with the claim that her moral status is affected by her luck that nothing bad happened. More precisely, one is agreeing with the proposition that she is morally less blameworthy for failing to look than Bert, other things being equal (or, alternatively, blameworthy for fewer states of affairs). In the eyes of the law, Bert is certainly more blameworthy than Carol, but is the same true in the moral court of law?

Some would argue, following Kant, that Bert's state of mind is, for all practical purposes, identical to Carol's. Why should the fortuitous fact that no one happened to run across Carol's driveway render her less morally blameworthy than Bert? Someone of Kant's persuasion will find the doctrine of moral luck utterly lacking in plausibility.

Here I admit that I have no knockdown argument against the Kantian position, but I will proceed on the assumption that Thomson is correct in thinking that moral luck is an undeniable feature of the moral landscape. The question now before us is how moral luck is relevant to the topic of accessory sin. The answer, I believe, is that moral luck can prevent one from becoming complicit in the sinful activity of another person.

The following are some ways in which moral luck can intervene to prevent a person from becoming complicit in the sinful behavior of another. First, the principal actor creates a plan to victimize an innocent person, a prospective accomplice agrees to participate, and the would-be victim moves to a distant location before the plan can be put into effect. Second, the principal actor engages in sinful behavior and asks someone else to cover for him. The person agrees but has no opportunity to do so because no one suspects the principal actor of having been involved. Third, the principal actor concocts a plan to engage in sinful behavior and then has a change of mind, thus preventing a would-be accomplice from becoming an actual accomplice. Fourth, the principal actor's devious plan attracts one would-be accomplice, but not enough additional accomplices can be found to put the plan into operation. Fifth, the principal actor's devious plan attracts enough participants, but they lack the skill required to bring about the harmful outcome they all desire.

In each of these cases someone might be perfectly willing to be an accomplice but, because of fortuitous events or circumstances, is prevented from doing so. To his or her way of thinking this course of events is a disappointment, but in reality he or she is experiencing moral luck and is thereby spared the moral blame that inevitably attaches to accessory sins, whether by commission or omission.

It is worth pointing out in closing that moral luck can prevent a person from sinning in circumstances other than an involvement in accessory sins. An individual planning to rob a bank without the assistance of anyone else might be prevented from doing so by the sudden appearance of a tornado. The individual, though probably disappointed, has been spared from committing a sin of serious proportions.

CHAPTER FOUR

MORTAL VERSUS
VENIAL SINS

Theologians have occasionally argued that all sins are equally serious from a moral perspective.[1] According to this view, one who commits the sin of thinking a lewd thought is every bit as guilty as one who sins by committing a capital crime. Moreover, one who commits a sin of omission is every bit as guilty as one performing any possible sin of commission.

The vast majority of those who have written about sin have rejected this point of view, holding that some sins are more serious than others. Moreover, in ordinary conversation people seem to agree that sins are not equally serious. This may be due in part to the fact that those convicted of crimes face penalties that differ widely in severity. Rare is the individual who would seriously maintain that all sins are equally serious.

The Catholic Church has taught for centuries that a distinction can be drawn between mortal (or cardinal) sins and venial sins, a view that appears to be clearly taught in the New Testament. In this chapter I will begin by discussing this distinction. The following section will explore in more general terms the thesis that some sins are more serious than others, morally speaking. In addition, I will discuss the potential this thesis holds for minimizing the seriousness of certain sins. The final section will take up the topic of the seven deadly sins.

MORTAL AND VENIAL SINS

I will begin this section by articulating the teachings of the Roman Catholic Church regarding the distinction between mortal and venial sins. Medieval philosophers such as Thomas Aquinas sometimes viewed sin as a sickness of the soul (*S. T.* I-II, Q. 88, 1894). Just as some physical diseases are mortal because they involve an irreparable defect, some sins are designated as mortal because the defect cannot be repaired. Mortal sins, then, are those that are irreparable. On the other hand, sins that are reparable are called venial sins. A sin receives its acquittal (veniam) when the debt of punishment is taken away, and when this happens the sin has been repaired. A venial sin does not entail anything to prevent its being pardoned.[2]

The Catholic Church teaches that sins should be evaluated according to their gravity. The distinction between mortal and venial sin is already present in scripture. "If you see any brother or sister commit a sin that does not lead to death, you should pray and God will give them life. I refer to those whose sin does not lead to death. There is a sin that leads to death. I am not saying that you should pray about that. All wrongdoing is sin, and there is sin that does not lead to death" (1 John 5:16–17). This distinction has become part of the Church's tradition. Mortal sin is a grave violation of God's law that destroys charity in the heart of human beings. It turns people away from God by preferring an inferior good to him. Venial sin, on the other hand, allows charity to subsist, even though it offends and wounds it.

Mortal sin attacks charity and necessitates a new conversion of the heart. This is normally accomplished through the sacrament of reconciliation.

For a sin to be mortal, three conditions must be satisfied. First, it is sin whose object is grave matter. What counts as grave matter is specified by the Ten Commandments and by Christ's answer to the rich young man in Matthew 19:16–22, who asks him what he must do to merit eternal life: "Do not kill, do not commit adultery, do not steal, do not bear false witness, do not defraud, honor your father and your mother." Second, mortal sin requires full knowledge. It presupposes knowledge of the sinful nature of the act and of its opposition to God's law. Third, it requires complete consent; it implies a consent sufficiently deliberate to be a personal choice.

Unintentional ignorance can mitigate or even remove the imputability of a grave offense; but no one can plead ignorance of the principles of the moral law, because they are contained in the conscience of every human being. Other factors, such as feelings, passions, and pathological disorder can reduce the voluntary and free character of the offense and its imputability. The gravest sin is that committed through malice by the deliberate choice of evil. Mortal sin results in the loss of charity and the privation of the state of grace. If it is not redeemed by repentance and God's forgiveness, it results in the eternal death of hell.

Venial sin is a less serious matter. We commit a venial sin when we do not observe the standard prescribed by the moral law or when we disobey the moral law in a grave manner but without full knowledge or complete consent. Venial sin weakens charity and manifests a disordered affection for created goods. It impedes our progress in the exercise of virtue and in the practice of moral good.

The deliberate commission of venial sin, if one does not repent of it, disposes us little by little to commit mortal sin. However, venial sin does not set us in direct opposition to the will of God, and it does not break our covenant with God. There are no limits to God's mercy, but anyone who deliberately refuses to accept his mercy rejects the forgiveness of sins. Such hardness of heart can lead to eternal loss of life and separation from God.[3]

Contemporary accounts of the distinction between mortal and venial sins characterize venial sins in terms of choosing wrong in some minor respect. For example, if one chooses the bad only in some minor respect, one has committed a venial sin, and one's will might remain focused on the good in respects recognized as more important. But if one deliberately chooses the bad in a respect recognized as important, one has committed a mortal sin, and one is setting oneself against the moral world (Swinburne 1989, 175–176).

Roman Catholic thinkers frequently approach the distinction between mortal and venial sins by introducing a distinction between major evils and minor evils. A major evil is characterized as one that strikes at the very dignity of the human being or one that involves the destruction of goods necessary for an individual or society. A minor evil is one that is not a major evil.

Based on this distinction, one can construct advice for persons wishing to live the moral life as follows: (1) perform no action in which any evil, major or minor, is willed as an end in itself; (2) perform no action in which any major evil is willed as a means to an end; (3) perform no action in which any minor evil is willed as a means to an end, unless there is a proportionate reason for doing so; (4) perform no action in which any of the risked side effects that are foreseen as possible are evil, unless there is a proportionate reason for doing so; and (5) perform no action that passes test (3) or (4) if there is an equally good method of attaining the same desired end but requires the performance of a lesser evil (Garrett 1966, 8–10).

Mortal sins emerge from this typology as those in which someone performs an action in which a major evil is willed as an end in itself or in which someone performs an action in which a major evil is willed as a means to an end. Venial sins constitute violations primarily involving minor evils.

THE UNEQUAL SERIOUSNESS OF SINS

Some thinkers reject the distinction between mortal and venial sins. And not all who acknowledge the distinction find it particularly useful or significant. But a great many philosophers and theologians endorse the idea that sins come in degrees. The thesis that some sins are more serious than others enjoys wide appeal. Few in modern times seem to champion the idea that all sins are equally serious or worthy of condemnation.[4]

According to Cornelius Plantinga, one might hold that all sins are equally wrong, but not all sins are equally bad. Many believe that thinking about adultery is just as wrong as committing it, but they also know that adultery in one's heart damages others less than committing it, and hence it can be regarded as less serious (C. Plantinga 1995, 21).

Plantinga believes that the badness or seriousness of a sin depends in part on the amount and kind of damage it inflicts, and this includes damage to the person committing the sin. Thus, it is less serious to covet a neighbor's property than to steal it. And it is less serious to neglect to expose one's children to the fine arts than to neglect to feed them. More will be said about Plantinga's distinction between a sin's being wrong and a sin's being bad in what follows.

The thesis that there are degrees of sin is common among world religions. Islam, for example, recognizes five gradations of sin. The lowest level is comprised of mistakes, the second level immorality, the third level transgressions, the fourth level wickedness and depravity, and the fifth level idolatry. Polytheism and ascribing a partner to God are also assigned to the fifth level.

Sometimes the idea that some sins are more serious than others is enshrined in doctrinal or confessional statements. The Second Helvetic Confession of 1562 states, "We confess that sins are not equal; although they arise from the same fountain of corruption and unbelief, some are more serious than others (chapter 8, as quoted by Plantinga 1995, 21n22)."

Here it is not my purpose to defend the claim that not all sins are equally serious from a moral point of view, for I believe that others have defended this claim to the point that virtually no one else would disagree. Rather, my concern is to warn of the potential for misuse of this doctrine. Under certain circumstances the belief that sins vary in their degree of seriousness could tempt one to believe that a particular sin is only minimally wrong when in fact it is significantly wrong.

Suppose that a man has been taught from a young age that all sins are equally serious. Convinced that impure thoughts are as bad as violent deeds, he has for many years exercised great self-control in erasing impure thoughts from his mind. In addition he has been extremely conscientious about guarding against sins of omission, making sure that he is never guilty of failing to do good deeds benefitting others. One day he reads chapter 8 of the Second Helvetic Confession and learns for the first time that sins are not equally momentous. He rejoices in the freedom and license that can now characterize his approach to living the moral life. No longer does he feel bound to banish impure thoughts from his mind, and no longer does he expend great time and energy worrying about sins of omission.

Perhaps many would agree that nothing is wrong with this change in his moral outlook. After all, his perspective at this juncture of his transition is not much different from the perspective that most of us embrace, at least implicitly. But suppose his thinking continues to evolve in the direction of freedom and license. Gradually, he begins to dismiss other barriers that have limited his thinking in the past. He accepts the idea, for example, that rudeness to others is not a sin of particular importance and that lying and cheating can be easily justified as sins that are trivial when compared to sins such as murder or sexual assault.

By now it is obvious that his judgment about the relative importance of various sins is becoming less and less reliable and that this transition is the result of learning that not all sins are equally serious. My only point thus far is that the doctrine that not all sins are equally serious has the potential for tempting one to suppose that there is no reason to be particularly concerned about sins that have the appearance of being minimal in importance.

Now let us carry this train of thought forward in a slightly different direction. Suppose that Plantinga is correct in thinking that sins can differ in terms of being bad and being wrong. Suppose further that sins can vary not only in terms of being bad but also in terms of being wrong. Then it is possible for a sin that is minimally bad to be significantly wrong, and it is possible for a sin that is minimally wrong to be significantly bad. Plantinga believes that the badness of sin varies according to the damage it causes. To use his examples, adultery can damage others, and neglecting to feed one's children can obviously inflict damage on them.

Suppose that the man in the previous example comes to believe that sins can vary in degrees of seriousness both in terms of how wrong they are and in terms of how bad they are. He pictures various potential sins as lying on a grid with one axis depicting how wrong they are and one axis depicting how bad they are, based on Plantinga's criteria for distinguishing them.[5] It would not be difficult to dismiss sins that score low on one axis even though they score high on the other. For example, a sin of depravity committed in the presence of no one else might score low on the scale of badness (although the man might damage himself slightly) and might for that reason be easy to justify. And the sin of neglecting to check his gasoline gauge might score low on the scale of wrongness even though the man runs out of fuel and several of his passengers miss crucial appointments. Once again, in his eyes this sin can be easily dismissed.

Next imagine a group of moral agents, each of whom operates according to the grid described in the previous paragraph. Sometimes the members of the group commit sins individually, and sometimes they commit sins in tandem with other members of the group (meaning that several of them are acting jointly to bring about a desired outcome). Over the course of time they discover a new method for rationalizing sins: When they commit sins in tandem with other members of the group, the score on the scale of badness can sometimes be distributed among the members with the result that each member's score is greatly diminished. In other circumstances, the score on the scale of wrongness can be distributed among the members with the result that each member's share is diminished.

Recall from chapter 3 an example in which three teenagers push a car into a lake. Suppose that the idea to push the car into the lake originates with two of the teenagers who know that the feat can be accomplished without the assistance of anyone else. In addition, they realize that performing such an action would be significantly sinful, particularly on the scale of badness. Mindful of this fact, they decide to recruit someone else to advance their plan. After a third teenager is persuaded to join them, the three push the car into the lake.

The two teenagers who initiate this course of events are convinced that the addition of the third participant reduces the degree of sin that can be assigned to each of them. And the addition of a fourth participant would further reduce the degree of sin assigned to each of them. They reason that if not all sins are equal, it makes perfect sense to speak of sin as admitting of degrees; thus adding participants can serve a useful purpose in reducing the degree of sin assigned to each of them.

However, one could challenge their assumption that, as the number of participants acting in tandem in a wrongful course of actions increases, the degree of sin assigned to each of them decreases. Challenging this assumption raises a larger question about sin: Is the amount of sin generated in a particular set of circumstances a constant that does not increase merely because additional participants become involved or decrease merely because fewer participants are involved? Here I shall only say that such an assumption appears dubious. Certainly many will be attracted to this particular way of thinking about sin and reducing the extent to which they are deserving of the judgment and condemnation of others (including, perhaps, a final judgment). I believe that many, in fact, hold a conception of sin not unlike what I have just been described. But it is hard to see what the basis or justification might be for such a conception of sin. Although I lack a decisive refutation of this view, I will tentatively conclude that, even though it enjoys a wide appeal in people's intuitive feelings about sin, it appears to lack a theoretical foundation.

THE SEVEN DEADLY SINS

In this section I will turn to another way in which the doctrine that not all sins are equal can be expressed. The idea that some sins are deadly and others are not has had a rich expression in historical writings as far back as the fourth century. While there have been differences in terms of which sins are deadly and which are not, as well as differences in the number of deadly sins, a remarkable consensus has emerged as to which sins have earned the designation of deadly. The account I present owes a considerable debt to the writings of Rebecca DeYoung.

The seven deadly sins are pride, envy, sloth, avarice, anger, lust, and gluttony. Pride, envy, and sloth are spiritual vices and concern spiritual goods such as love for others or love for God. Avarice and anger have to do with goods such as power, honor, and justice. Lust and gluttony deal with bodily pleasures (DeYoung 2008, 25).

For most of their history, the seven deadly sins were known as the seven capital vices (ibid.). They are mentioned as far back as Evagrius Ponticus, who lived from 346 until 399. Gregory the Great explained and discussed them in his *Moralia in Iob* (trans as *Morals on the Book of Job*, 1844), and they were given a more systematic treatment by scholastic writers in the thirteenth century.

The list did not remain the same throughout history. Evagrius's original list actually included eight: sloth, sadness, vainglory, pride, avarice, anger, lust, and gluttony. Gregory the Great also acknowledged eight, but his list differed from that of Evagrius in adding envy and in regarding sloth as a form of sadness. On the basis of a passage in Sirach stating that pride is the beginning of all sin, Gregory regarded pride as the chief vice and the other seven as offshoots. His list achieved an authoritative status that it held for centuries.

Once pride came to be acknowledged as the chief vice, illustrators began to picture the sins as a tree with seven main branches. The sin of pride formed the root from which the other seven grew as the main branches. Other sins were then depicted as offshoots and fruit growing from these branches. Picturing the sins in this manner enabled people to see that the ultimate source of sin was pride. An attack on the sin of pride could then be considered as an attack on the rest.

Over the course of time, the list of sins diminished from eight to seven. With the realization that vainglory was similar to pride, vainglory was dropped from the list. Another change that took place was that sadness was replaced with sloth. The list that is recognized as authoritative by scholars in the present time is pride, envy, sloth, avarice, anger, lust, and gluttony.

The "corresponding" list of seven virtues began with the three cardinal virtues of faith, hope, and charity (love) and also included prudence, justice, courage, and temperance. The first three are articulated in 1 Corinthians 13:13, and the last four (the four classical Greek virtues) are articulated in Wisdom 8:7. One should not look for a direct correlation between the seven deadly sins and the seven virtues. The virtue that opposes pride is humility, a virtue that does not appear on the list.

It is worth repeating that the seven deadly sins were originally known as the seven capital vices. This of course raises the question as to the precise relationship between sins and vices. Perhaps the relationship can be stated as follows: Whenever the practice of a moral vice takes place, it counts as a sin, but not every sin is necessarily the instantiation of a moral vice. More will be said about the relationship between sin and vice in chapters 8 and 9.

CHAPTER FIVE

SUPEREROGATION
AND SIN

An act of supererogation is standardly defined as an act that satisfies three conditions: (1) one who performs the act is morally praiseworthy, (2) it fulfills no moral obligations, and (3) one is not morally blameworthy for omitting it. Roughly speaking, one goes beyond the call of duty when one performs an act of supererogation.

There are several ways in which the notion of supererogation is relevant to the topic of sin. First, if it is one's duty or obligation to act in a manner that is morally praiseworthy, as many believe, then it would appear that acts of supererogation are not possible. For if one inevitably has a duty or obligation to do what is morally praiseworthy, then no act can possibly fulfill both conditions 1 and 2 above. Thus, if the failure to do what is one's duty or obligation constitutes sinful behavior, on the supposition that one always has an obligation to act in a praiseworthy manner, it is always sinful not to act in a praiseworthy manner. Whenever one has the opportunity to perform a praiseworthy act, one has an obligation to do so, and the failure to do so is sinful.

Second, if people are as sinful as is commonly believed, it might seem unlikely that they are capable of truly praiseworthy behavior that is beyond the call of duty. In particular, a commitment to the notion of original sin might lead one to a position of skepticism regarding the possibility of performing acts of supererogation.

Third, one is never morally blameworthy for omitting the performance of an act of supererogation. However, one can be morally blameworthy and hence sinful if one repeatedly passes up opportunities to perform acts of supererogation. In addition, it can be sinful to omit performing an act of supererogation if one's underlying motives are sufficiently sinister or depraved. Examples of both phenomena will be provided in what follows.

No doubt there are additional ways in which the concept of supererogation is relevant to issues involving sin, but I shall restrict the discussion in this chapter to the three listed here. In the final section I will briefly introduce the concept of quasi-supererogation and explain its relevance to sin, and in the appendix I will address questions about heaven.

SUPEREROGATION IS NOT POSSIBLE

For centuries there has been a great deal of opposition to the thesis that acts of supererogation are possible. This opposition has usually taken the form of insisting that, whenever one has an opportunity to perform an act that is morally praiseworthy, it is wrong or sinful not to perform the act. Thus, conditions 1 through 3 cannot jointly be satisfied.

The story of this opposition begins with the sale of indulgences by some individuals within the Holy Catholic Church, such as the German Dominican Johann Tetzel (1465–1519). The purchase of an indulgence was a means to lessen the punishment in the afterlife of those who have sinned in this life. Certain dioceses in the Church profited handsomely from this arrangement, and over time it degenerated into a practice beset with corruption. The principle underlying the sale of indulgences was that Jesus Christ and certain saints had, through their exemplary lives, built up a treasury of good works. It was believed possible for a measure of their accrued merit to be applied to the accounts of ordinary sinners, and their penalty in the afterlife could in this manner be lessened. A few people manage to end their lives with a surplus of good, and this makes possible the lessening of penalties applied to others. Certain individuals in the Church were given the task of administering these penalties to make certain that the overall balance sheets of these sinners remained intact.

The reformers Martin Luther, John Calvin, and Philip Melanchton vigorously objected to the idea that a treasury of merit, conceived in this manner, is possible and can be applied to the accounts of ordinary sinners. According to them, it is always sinful to fail to do good works. Luther, in particular, asserted that whenever a good work is performed, the person doing it is simply doing what God has commanded. Even the saints, according to Luther, have done nothing that is superabundant. Everything they have done is obligatory; even their acts of martyrdom are obligatory (Luther 1943, 213). Clearly, for the reformers there is no possibility that the works of human moral agents can constitute any type of treasury of merit, and there is no possibility that human moral agents can perform acts of supererogation.

These sentiments are echoed in the Episcopalians' 1559 *Book of Common Prayer*. In article 14, acts of supererogation are explicitly rejected on the grounds that there can be no voluntary works over and above God's commandments.

Various influential twentieth-century thinkers followed squarely in this tradition. One type of view focuses on the concept of perfection. God calls all of us to live lives of perfection, and hence it is not only our duty to strive for perfection; it is also our duty to attain perfection (Rahner 1965, 48–49). It is hard to see how there can be any room here for supererogation. There is no such thing as attaining perfection, thereby fulfilling a duty, and then proceeding to perform a meritorious work over and above the perfection one has attained.

Others follow in this same tradition by commenting on an example from J. O. Urmson in which a soldier falls on a live grenade in order to save his comrades. Urmson believes that this is a paradigmatic example of a supererogatory act. It can be argued, however, that according to the strict requirements of covenantal love, the soldier did what he should have done. More generally, if under the strict requirements of covenantal love a person should have gone a second mile, then the person can be blamed for not having done so (Allen 1984, 127). Once again, acts of supererogation are ruled out, and it is sinful not to have gone the second mile.

Many other philosophers have taken an anti-supererogationist stance, affirming that one is always blameworthy or sinful for failing to do what is praiseworthy or meritorious. Kantian ethics are widely believed to be anti-supererogationist. W. D. Ross, who follows in the Kantian tradition, asserts in his book *The Right and the Good* that it is self-evident that if there are things that are intrinsically good, it is our prima facie duty to bring them into existence and to bring as many of them into existence as possible (Ross 1973, 24).

Some versions of act utilitarianism (the view that one ought always do the greatest good for the greatest number) likewise rule out the possibility of performing acts of supererogation. Roughly speaking, if one is at all times morally obligated to bring about the greatest benefits to the greatest number, it will be challenging to find a way to do something praiseworthy that is not at the same time an obligation. Fred Feldman adopts a "neo-utilitarian" view based on a possible-worlds approach. It requires a person to do what he or she would do in the best possible worlds accessible to the actual world. Others argue on utilitarian grounds that we have a duty not just to make civilized life possible but also to make it as good as we are able. Saints and heroes go to extraordinary lengths to bring about good in human life. But, according to Christopher New (New 1974, 183), contrary to what Urmson has alleged (Urmson 1969), saints and heroes are only doing their duty. Saintly people will frequently say that they are only doing their duty and will regard their having done any less as sinful. Many other act utilitarians have articulated views that are anti-supererogationist in nature.

Some versions of ethical prescriptivism leave no room for acts of supererogation. Some argue on prescriptivist grounds that saintly and heroic acts are not properly classified as supererogatory; rather, they are properly classified as obligatory (Pybus 1982, 195). Aspiring to be the sorts of persons saintly or heroic persons are is what we ought to be doing.

A great many philosophers have taken an anti-supererogationist position for a variety of reasons. Not all of these philosophers have made specific reference to sin. But if one believes that there is such a thing as sin, one will no doubt hold that the failure to do one's duty is sinful and hence that if the category of praiseworthy acts is completely swallowed up by moral obligation, it is sinful to forgo an opportunity to perform a praiseworthy act.

Those who defend the possibility of actions qualifying as acts of supererogation might appeal to the ethical principle, which enjoys almost universal acceptance, that "ought" implies "can." According to this principle, one has a moral duty to perform an act only if one is able to perform it. In other words, if one is not able to perform an act, one has no moral obligation to perform it.

One who denies the possibility of supererogation for human moral agents (for the reasons just cited) appears committed to the denial of the ought-implies-can principle.[1] Suppose that a man has a ten-dollar bill and no other cash as he walks down the street. He passes two homeless persons asking for money. It would be morally praiseworthy to give the ten-dollar bill to the first person, and it would be morally praiseworthy to give it to the second person. According to the principle that every praiseworthy act is obligatory, he has an obligation to give the ten-dollar bill to both persons. But since doing so is impossible, the principle that "ought" implies can is violated.

OUR SINFUL NATURE PRECLUDES ACTS OF SUPEREROGATION

In the previous section I examined the claim that acts of supererogation are not possible on the grounds that every act that is morally praiseworthy is at the same time morally obligatory. This section takes up the claim that, because human moral agents are sinful by nature, they can rarely if ever perform praiseworthy acts that are above and beyond the call of duty. Perhaps human beings are capable of performing acts that are mildly praiseworthy, but these are not the sorts of acts that transcend duty.

The view under examination here differs from that surveyed in the previous section in that it allows that some morally praiseworthy acts are not at the same time morally obligatory. The problem is that these acts are praiseworthy to such a degree that people, because of their sinful nature, are rarely if ever capable of performing them.

The doctrine of original sin, roughly stated, affirms that we have inherited a sinful nature. Naturally, this condition affects our desire and ability to act in a morally praiseworthy manner. As such, this doctrine does not preclude our performing acts of supererogation. But recall from chapter 2 that some adherents to the doctrine of original sin claim that our depravity is total or complete. Certainly those who affirm the doctrine of total depravity will judge that human beings, left to their own devices, will rarely if ever perform praiseworthy acts, let alone praiseworthy acts that rise above and beyond the call of duty.

It should be noted that adherents to the doctrine of total depravity typically believe in addition that people can, with outside help, escape this deplorable state and thereby perform acts that are morally praiseworthy—and even acts that are significantly praiseworthy. Two Reformed confessional statements of the sixteenth century, the 1562 Belgic Confession and the 1563 Heidelberg Catechism, teach not only that all human moral agents suffer from total depravity but that these same moral agents can be delivered from this state through grace.

Nevertheless, left to their own devices, those who suffer from total depravity appear to be dubious prospects for performing acts of supererogation. Even if they are capable of performing acts for which they are mildly blameworthy—and this is by no means clearly compatible with the doctrine of total depravity—their prospects of being able to perform significantly praiseworthy acts seems vanishingly small. And this does not bode well for their prospects of being able to perform acts of supererogation. From all appearances, those who suffer from total depravity, left to their own resources, lack the ability to perform acts of supererogation.

It is worth pointing out that not all acts of supererogation are significantly praiseworthy. Discussions of supererogation commonly leave the impression that typical examples of supererogation involve behavior that is saintly or based on heroic self-sacrifice. Urmson's famous 1969 essay, "Saints and Heroes," has exerted tremendous influence on how people think about the place of supererogation in their moral lives. Performing acts that are above and beyond the call of duty conjures up images of noble deeds that are anything but trivially praiseworthy.

Rarely has it been pointed out in the literature that actions for which one would be minimally praiseworthy can sometimes qualify as supererogatory. Buying lunch for a co-worker who has inadvertently left his wallet at home appears to be a strong candidate for qualifying as an act of supererogation. Performing such an act is certainly not praiseworthy to a high degree, but it is mildly praiseworthy. Moreover, it does not seem to be obligatory, nor does its omission seem to be morally blameworthy or sinful. I contend that this qualifies as an act of supererogation. Perhaps not everyone will be convinced by this particular example, but there are many others, such as offering to cover the office phone while everyone else is downstairs at the office Christmas party. Small acts of kindness, depending on the circumstances, can qualify as acts of supererogation.

The fact that performing some acts of supererogation is praiseworthy to only a modest or minimal degree does not, of course, settle the question of whether the doctrine of total depravity is compatible with the ability to perform acts of supererogation. A proponent of this doctrine might well contend that performing even minimally praiseworthy acts is beyond the reach of someone suffering from total depravity (that is, someone who has not sought assistance from the outside). But those who allow that human beings are at least capable of performing modestly praiseworthy acts can affirm that it is possible to perform acts of supererogation. One committed to the doctrine of original sin need not, therefore, feel compelled to reject the possibility of performing acts of supererogation, at least not for the reasons articulated in this section.

OMITTING ACTS OF SUPEREROGATION IS NOT A SIN

One is not morally blameworthy or sinful for omitting acts of supererogation, by definition. The previous sections of this chapter dealt with the fact that one is praiseworthy for performing acts of supererogation, by definition, and also the fact that, by definition, it is not obligatory to perform them. In this section we focus on the third condition of the definition of supererogation, the one that states that a person is not blameworthy for declining to perform an act of supererogation.

Suppose that someone is in a position to perform an act of supererogation and decides not to do so. In such a case it would be unfair for someone else to criticize the person for not doing do ("You could have given that co-worker money for his lunch; shame on you that someone else had to do so" or "Passing by that beggar on the street was a sin for which you will one day be held accountable"). Perhaps in such a situation the moral blame rests with the accuser, not the accused.

Nevertheless, one can be morally blameworthy for repeatedly declining opportunities to perform acts of supererogation. Moreover, one can be sinful for omitting to perform an act of supererogation if one's motives are sufficiently sinister. In this section I will provide examples of both phenomena. In the course of explaining the second phenomenon I will draw on the work of Gregory Trianosky.

Although one is never blameworthy for declining to perform an act of supererogation, one can be blameworthy or sinful for declining many potential acts of supererogation over an extended period of time. Suppose that someone who regularly attends Mass never gives money when the collection plate for benevolence is passed. On a given occasion this person might argue that donating to benevolence is an act of supererogation, and we might wholeheartedly agree. But if this person were to argue that never donating to benevolence is simply declining to do what is supererogatory, we might well become skeptical.

One way to picture this situation is to think about disjunctive actions. There is the action of giving on the first opportunity, the action of giving on the second opportunity, the action of giving on the third opportunity, and so forth. Now consider the disjunctive action of giving on the first opportunity, giving on the second opportunity, giving on the third opportunity, or so forth. From the fact that each individual disjunct constitutes one's declining to perform an act of supererogation, it does not follow that the disjunction itself constitutes one's declining to perform an act of supererogation. Hence it may well be that failing to perform the disjunctive action itself is morally blameworthy or sinful.

Let us now consider the possibility that declining to perform an act of supererogation can be sinful if one's motives are sinister or depraved. Here I believe that an excursion into the realm of virtue ethics can be illuminating, and I appeal to Gregory Trianosky's article "Supererogation, Wrongdoing, and Vice: On the Autonomy of the Ethics of Virtue."

Trianosky notes that people often make excuses for failing to perform acts of supererogation. When others challenge them to go the second mile and they decline, they frequently experience discomfort or shame and feel the need to make excuses. But Trianosky finds this puzzling, for there is no logical reason for them to make excuses. Since they are not morally blameworthy for failing to perform acts of supererogation, it is perfectly appropriate to say "No thanks" when others challenge one to perform such an act.

Trianosky explains why people feel the need to make excuses in these situations by drawing a distinction between two types of negative moral judgments. Negative deontic judgments concern the wrongness of someone's performing or neglecting to perform some particular act. Negative aretaic judgments are judgments about a conative or affective state of the person involved.[2] Trianosky believes that there are two kinds of negative aretaic judgments. Some are judgments about the viciousness of standing traits or dispositions, and others are judgments about the viciousness of occurrent motives or states. An example of the first type is a judgment about how cowardly someone is. An example of the second type is a judgment about how inconsiderate someone was on some particular occasion.

A person failing to perform an act of supererogation can never be deserving of a negative deontic judgment, for he or she is not morally blameworthy as such in declining to perform an act of supererogation. But just because declining to perform an act of supererogation is never deserving of a negative deontic judgment, Trianosky emphasizes, one cannot infer that he or she is not deserving of a negative aretaic judgment. He believes, in fact, that one is often susceptible to a negative aretaic judgment. This can take place when one's failure to act results from a motive that is less than virtuous.

On occasion, people find themselves with an opportunity to benefit others and react with total indifference. It is one thing to react with indifference to the needs of others when declining to perform an act of supererogation. It is quite another thing to react with regret and concern for those one declines to assist when failing to perform an act of supererogation. According to Trianosky, when indifference characterizes one's electing not to act, it is reasonable to judge that the omission is the result of a nonvirtuous state of mind and that a negative aretaic judgment is appropriate.

Sometimes a person's declining to perform an act of supererogation is the result of a vicious motive. For example, it may be out of spite that one elects to withhold a benefit from someone else. It might be that someone experiences a perverse pleasure from withholding such a benefit, and that is his or her reason for doing so. In such cases the motives underlying his or her declining to perform an act of supererogation can appropriately be criticized, and this type of criticism takes the form of a negative aretaic judgment.

Recall that people feel the need to offer excuses when declining to perform acts of supererogation, and recall, too, that Trianosky finds this puzzling. Now an explanation for this puzzling phenomenon presents itself. People believe that when they decline to perform acts of supererogation others might judge their omission as the result of motives that are less than virtuous, or even vicious, and for this reason they make excuses for failing to act. When others become suspicious that their motives are less than virtuous, those omitting to perform acts of supererogation believe it is important to assure them that their motives are not morally deficient.

People do not offer these excuses, Trianosky believes, to deflect or forestall negative deontic judgments, for there is no rational point in doing so. Once again, one is not morally blameworthy in declining to perform an act of supererogation. These excuses, rather, are offered to forestall negative aretaic judgments for fear that others will suspect that the omission is the result of a state of mind that is less than virtuous. People often decline to perform acts of supererogation in states of mind that are nonvirtuous, and for this reason Trianosky believes that people will understandably suspect on occasion that these states of mind give rise to such omissions.

Trianosky does not mention sin as an ingredient or factor in one's declining to perform an act of supererogation. But surely one could plausibly judge that a vicious motive that produces such an omission is a sinful motive. In addition, depending on the circumstances, a nonvirtuous motive that leads one to decline to perform an act of supererogation, a motive that warrants a negative aretaic judgment, can at the same time qualify as a sinful motive. This is not to say that whenever a negative aretaic judgment is appropriate a sinful motive is the root cause, but many of the situations Trianosky has in mind can plausibly be identified as involving sinful motives.

QUASI-SUPEREROGATION IS DIFFERENT FROM SUPEREROGATION

An act of quasi-supererogation differs from an act of supererogation in that one is morally blameworthy or sinful if one omits doing it. The definition of an act of quasi-supererogation, accordingly, is as follows: (1) One is morally praiseworthy for performing it, (2) it fulfills no moral obligations, and (3) one is blameworthy or sinful for omitting it.

It might initially seem unlikely that any act can satisfy all three conditions. How can the same act that one is praiseworthy to perform be blameworthy to omit? The answer, I believe, is that one is mildly praiseworthy for performing some acts are and mildly blameworthy for omitting them. Certainly an act of heroic self-sacrifice that one is significantly praiseworthy for performing will not be one that a person is blameworthy for omitting, but it is possible for an act that one is mildly praiseworthy for performing to be one that he or she is blameworthy or sinful for omitting.

Consider, for example, a man's overcoming a strong temptation to physically harm someone who has harmed him. It is not difficult to imagine that overcoming this strong temptation can be morally praiseworthy. At the same time, it is reasonable to suppose that harming someone in an act of revenge can be sinful. Situations of this type are sometimes called morally charged states of affairs.

The harm in question need not be physical harm. Suppose that a man is having dinner with his disabled wife in a restaurant and a man at the next table is making loud jokes and mocking gestures about her physical disabilities. Surely her husband will be strongly tempted to say something mean-spirited or profane to the man at the next table and he would be morally praiseworthy for resisting this temptation. On the other hand, were he to give in to this temptation, his verbal abuse would arguably qualify as making him blameworthy to at least a modest degree.

One might wonder whether a discussion of quasi-supererogation makes a contribution to our understanding of sin sufficient to warrant a section of its own. Here it is worth pointing out that human moral agents sometimes encounter morally charged situations in which the only way to avoid sinful behavior is to do that which is morally praiseworthy (or to omit such an act in a manner for which he is praiseworthy). In a morally charged situation, there is no morally neutral option, and it is important for a person who is conscientious about leading a moral life to recognize this fact, a fact that is rarely if ever pointed out in discussions about sin. Perhaps situations involving strong temptations comprise paradigmatic examples of morally charged states of affairs, but other examples might take the form of honoring promises made on the basis of false or misleading information supplied by others. More will be said in the following chapter about morally charged situations.

APPENDIX

Those who believe that there is such a place as heaven have generally assumed that those who dwell there are sinless. Once a person has departed from this life and entered heaven, the person ceases to commit sins. Traditional teachings about heaven also include the idea that those who have gone to heaven grow in grace over the course of time. But how are these teachings compatible? How can one grow in grace if one is sinless to begin with?

One suggestion is that the inhabitants of heaven are capable of performing acts of supererogation. According to this idea, these people can perform acts for which they will be morally praiseworthy though the acts are not morally required. If they decline to perform these acts, they have done nothing for which they are morally blameworthy as such. Hence, they will remain sinless if they decline to perform these acts (Pawl and Timpe 2009, 414–415).

Now praiseworthiness is capable of coming in degrees. One is slightly praiseworthy for performing some acts, moderately praiseworthy for performing others, and still other acts are highly praiseworthy to perform. Inhabitants of heaven can begin their sojourns by performing acts of supererogation for which they will be modestly praiseworthy. Over the course of time they can progress to acts of supererogation for which they will be slightly more praiseworthy, then, over longer periods of time, to acts of supererogation for which they will have still higher levels of praiseworthiness, and so forth. In this way they can be said to grow in grace in spite of a sinless existence. It might be objected that they should proceed to higher levels of praiseworthiness as soon as possible. But this objection flies in the face of the basic nature of supererogation, according to which one is not the least bit blameworthy for declining to perform an act of supererogation. Therefore, one is not the least bit blameworthy for performing an act of supererogation with a modest rather than a substantial level of praiseworthiness.

CHAPTER SIX

THE ISLAMIC CATEGORY
OF ACTS THAT ARE
DISCOURAGED

The divine command theory of morality, roughly speaking, states that morally wrong actions are determined by what violates the commands of God, and actions that do not violate the commands of God are morally permissible. A person who subscribes to this theory of morality will find it natural to think of sin as that which violates the commands of God. A sin of commission will consist of doing what is prohibited by the commands of God, and a sin of omission will consist of failing to do what God commands that one do. Of course, people might have differences of opinion as to what exactly God is commanding them to do or to refrain from doing, but this is at least how the divine command theory of morality suggests that one think about sin.

Those who subscribe to the divine command theory might disagree as to whether these are the *only* sins that people are capable of committing. Can there be sins that do not in any manner violate the commands of God? Some interesting perspectives on this question can be found in a number of Islamic codes of ethics. One such code divides actions into five basic moral categories: the required, the forbidden, the recommended, the discouraged, and the permitted.

Certainly it is a sin, from the perspective of the divine command theory, to fail to do what is required by God. But consider the fourth category, the discouraged (Muslim jurists differ about which actions to include in this category). Could it not be a sin to commit acts that are discouraged by God? Could these not consist of acts that it is bad to perform but not forbidden? If there are acts that God discourages but does not forbid moral agents to perform, one might feel inclined to judge that it is a sin to perform one of these acts. To put it another way, it can be sinful to do what God discourages one from doing.

In the remainder of this chapter I will examine a category of acts to which Julia Driver calls attention (1992), acts that she believes capture the spirit of the Islamic category of the discouraged. I will then explore in detail the view that sinful behavior can take the form of doing what God discourages one from doing. Since it is relatively uncontroversial to claim that violating God's commandments is sinful, I will not defend this claim. With regard to the five basic moral categories of the Islamic code, it is relatively uncontroversial to claim that failing to do what is required is sinful and doing what is forbidden is likewise sinful. In what follows I will concentrate on the more ambiguous case of the discouraged. In the second section I will make reference, in addition, to behavior God encourages us to engage in. The final section explores the connection between sin and what we are discouraged from doing.

SUBEROGATORY ACTS

In her insightful article "The Suberogatory," Julia Driver makes a persuasive case for what she calls suberogatory acts. She characterizes them as acts that it is bad to perform although not forbidden—or, in other words, acts that are worse than a situation calls for but not forbidden. She describes them later in the article as permissible though bad. By describing them as permissible, she is implying that they do not violate moral duty.

By characterizing suberogatory acts as bad, I believe that Driver regards people performing them as worthy of moral blame. In one of her examples, there is only one place in a crowded train where two unoccupied seats are together. A man entering the train just ahead of a married couple assumes they wish to sit together and is considering whether to sit in one of the two unoccupied seats. Driver asserts that he would be blameworthy for taking one of these seats instead of taking a less convenient seat for himself. Taking one of these seats, in her opinion, would be a subererogatory act.

Driver observes that, roughly speaking, the Islamic category of the recommended corresponds to the category of supererogation and the Islamic category of the discouraged corresponds to the category of the suberogatory. Since suberogatory acts are also permissible, one might be tempted to judge that they also correspond to the fifth Islamic category, the permitted. But it seems prudent to regard the fifth category as comprising only those permitted acts that fail to be included in the previous four categories. Thus, they are permitted acts that are classified neither with the recommended nor with the discouraged. Absentmindedly scratching one's ear would be an example of such an act.

In chapter 2, acts of offence were introduced as acts for which people are morally blameworthy but are not morally forbidden, and one might easily conclude that they are exactly the same as suberogatory acts. However, there is a slight difference: While it is not praiseworthy to omit acts of offence, it is possible for it to be praiseworthy to omit suberogatory acts. The man entering the train ahead of the married couple might take a less convenient seat for himself, and, according to Driver, he would be praiseworthy for doing so. From this it follows that if he takes the course of action for which he would be blameworthy, it would not be an act of offence.

Since it distinguishes between the category of the forbidden and the category of the discouraged, the Islamic code of ethics opens the door to the possibility of acts that are morally substandard but do not violate obligation. When a person is morally discouraged from performing an act, the act is no doubt something for which he or she would be morally blameworthy. Since an act of this type is distinguished from an act that is morally forbidden, Driver seems correct in judging that the category of the discouraged roughly corresponds to the category of the suberogatory.

Driver does not make reference to that which God commands or discourages, but on the basis of what she argues we can perhaps conclude that acts God discourages are acts that qualify as suberogatory.

MORAL EXPECTATION

In this section I will introduce the notion of moral expectation. It will be my contention that doing what God discourages one from doing is roughly the same as failing to do what God expects but does not command one to do. Thus, to the extent that one sins by not fulfilling God's expectations, one sins by doing what God discourages. In the remainder of this section I will not speak explicitly about sin as the failure to fulfill God's expectations; I will operate on the assumption that such failure constitutes sin sometimes but not always.

Living a conscientious moral life involves acting in accord with one's moral expectations. When others (or even we ourselves) form moral expectations about what we will do, these expectations are often regarded as significant. Frequently we act on the basis of moral expectations and subsequently judge that we have done what we are rightly expected to do. In this way, acting on the basis of moral expectations is often a moral reason for what we do. Moral education involves learning what is morally expected of us by those in our family or community.

It is important to establish at the outset that moral expectation is not the same as moral obligation. While we can be morally expected to do what we are morally obligated to do, the reverse is not true. Sometimes the fulfillment of a moral expectation is not at the same time the fulfillment of a moral obligation. Imagine standing just inside the entrance to a store during a heavy downpour of rain and observing a woman arriving with her arms full of packages. While you might have no moral obligation to open the door for her, surely you can be morally expected to do so.

The relation between moral expectation and the category of the discouraged is that the failure to do what is morally expected of us is discouraged but not forbidden (unless we are at the same time violating a moral obligation). Thus, you would be morally discouraged from not opening the door for the woman, but such a failure would not be morally forbidden. It is also important to recognize that moral expectation differs from epistemic expectation. A college student might form an expectation, based on past experience, that her roommate will drink coffee every morning, but there is no moral dimension to this expectation. It is an expectation of an epistemic nature.

The failure to live up to one's moral expectations always makes one morally blameworthy to at least a modest or minimal degree, whereas the failure to carry out one's moral obligations, other things being equal, makes one blameworthy to a greater degree. Your failure to open the door for the woman makes you blameworthy to a minimal degree, but if the failure had been a violation of a moral duty (say, if you were an employee and the store owner had instructed you to do so), you would be blameworthy for your failure to a significant degree.

We are not always morally expected to live up to a moral expectation formed by someone else. Suppose that someone is drowning at a public beach. I cannot swim, but a person on the beach mistakenly believes that I will come to the rescue of the drowning individual. On this basis, the person forms a moral expectation that I perform the rescue. Nevertheless, in this situation I am not morally expected to perform the rescue. The person on the beach is mistaken to have formed this moral expectation of me, and therefore it is a false moral expectation.

It is reasonable to suppose that God forms moral expectations regarding our lives and that these are never false moral expectations. What God commands us to do are moral requirements; we are morally obligated to do what he commands us to do. But when God forms an expectation that a person will act in a certain way without simultaneously commanding the person to do so, the expectation is not false, and the person is morally blameworthy for his or her failure to act in this way is. And when God expects a person to refrain from acting in a particular manner and does not simultaneously command the person not to act, the person is morally blameworthy for failing to act in that manner.

In those instances in which God expects a person to refrain from acting, it is plausible to judge that God discourages the person from acting. Therefore, God's expectations can be linked to the Islamic category of the discouraged. An act that God expects a person not to perform is an act that God discourages the person from performing, and an act that God expects a person to perform is an act that God discourages a person to refrain from performing. The viewpoint that God expresses his will in ways other than commands has a fair amount of historical precedent. A distinction between the commandments of God and the counsels of God was maintained by some scholastic philosophers. St. Thomas Aquinas, for example, held that a commandment of God was obligatory, whereas a counsel of God was optional. The decision whether or not to perform an act is optional for someone if God counsels him or her to perform it. But the decision whether or not to perform an act is never optional if it is an act that God has commanded (*S. T.*, IaIIae, Q. 108, Art. 4).

Aquinas draws a distinction between the Old Law and the New Law (ibid.). The Old Law, the law of bondage, contains God's commands exclusively. The New Law, or the law of liberty, is composed of both God's commands and God's counsels. It is fitting to respond to God's counsels in a spirit of liberty, whereas Aquinas believes this is not the case when responding to God's commands. In addition, he stresses that God intends his counsels to benefit those who fulfill them. They are supremely useful, and it is in our best interests to carry them out. While we are at liberty to carry them out or not, declining to do so is the more foolish choice.

The counsels of God, as Aquinas describes them, are directed to people in several areas of their lives, namely, areas relating to wealth, carnal pleasures, and honors. We are counseled by God to renounce wealth, carnal pleasures, and pride. A person who entirely renounces these will embark on a life of poverty, chastity, and obedience. Of course, no one is obligated to lead such a life, but the more one renounces wealth, carnal pleasures, and pride, the more Aquinas believes we are acting in our best interests. The more that we renounce them, the closer we become to attaining eternal happiness. The counsels of God are described as optional recommendations, and God's intent is to benefit those who carry them out.

It is important to note that counsels are not the same as expectations. What they have in common is that they are optional; omitting their performance is not morally forbidden. But Aquinas does not indicate that one who omits the performance of a counsel is morally blameworthy. Conceivably, on some occasions a person's failure to carry out a counsel of God may be morally blameworthy. However, one is not always morally blameworthy if one fails to carry out a counsel of God. If someone fails to live a life of poverty or chastity, he or she is not deserving of blame for that reason. While one is always morally blameworthy for failing to live up to moral expectations, the same is not true of counsels.

The scholastic concept of a counsel can perhaps be judged as comparable to the Islamic category of the recommended. Acts that are recommended are neither required nor (merely) permitted. Performing them is good, not required, and there is nothing wrong with failing to perform them.

Why is this scholastic distinction important for understanding God's expectations? The answer is that it emphasizes the place of human liberty in the process of deciding how to react to God's will. Suppose that God expressed his will solely by way of commands. In that case there would be no opportunity for humans to respond in an optional manner. Naturally, we are able to disobey the commands of God, and this might give us the feeling of liberty. But this is not the kind of liberty that Aquinas describes. The liberty he has in mind is being able to refrain from acting without having to face punishment.

The law of liberty is what Aquinas calls "moral law," which is composed of both counsels and commands. We have the liberty to decide whether or not to act in accord with God's counsels and are encouraged to live up to these counsels because doing so is beneficial to us. But we are free to refrain from doing so. Refraining carries with it no penalty. Such a system of moral law does not necessarily mean that God forms (non-obligatory) moral expectations of persons. But it does embody an important ingredient for making expectations possible—liberty in response to God's will.

Viewing these ideas in a slightly different manner, if God has reason to encourage us toward certain kinds of activity, it is plausible to suppose that he has reason to discourage us from other kinds of activity. A theory that embraces both his encouragement and his discouragement is a theory that encompasses both his counsels and expectations.

A theory that encompasses only what God commands or forbids has no place for what he encourages or discourages (apart from what he commands) and invites the idea of God as a disciplinarian who is stern. Aquinas, on the other hand, paints the picture of a God who encourages us to act in accord with his counsels, counsels that are intended to benefit us. This is the picture of a caring God, a God who gives us the gift of liberty, a liberty that is more extensive than the freedom to disobey. The God he describes disciplines those who disobey his commands, but in addition he counsels them to act in such a way as to benefit them. And just as he encourages us to perform actions that are not required, he discourages others that are not forbidden. And just as his encouragement of certain actions in the account of Aquinas embodies caring, it is possible that his discouragement of certain other actions embodies a concern that is caring.

I believe that Aquinas likely agrees that God's discouragement, similar to his encouragement, stems from a caring concern. There are two types of moral duty in Aquinas (*S.T.*, IaIIae, 99, Art. 5). One type exists when reason teaches that a certain activity should take place to guarantee the order of virtue. A second type of duty exists when reason teaches that a certain activity is useful for the order of virtue. The second type does not involve any kind of command or prohibition, and hence it is not forbidden not to perform it. From God's point of view, not performing it may well be discouraged.

If God knows that acting in accord with his counsels is in our best interests, it is reasonable to hold that God knows that acting in accord with his expectations in also in our best interests. Since he designs his counsels with our best interests in mind, it does not seem plausible to suppose that he designs his expectations to have a detrimental impact on us. This is not necessarily to say that his expectations are designed to benefit us, but it seems likely that God believes his expectations, when carried out, will serve some type of worthwhile purpose. And this suggests that God's creating moral expectations for us suggests a caring concern on God's part and that whether or not we carry them out is something to which he is not indifferent.

Earlier we saw that God discourages people from failing to fulfill his expectations, and it is reasonable to suppose that he is disappointed when they do fail to do so. The situation differs from failing to carry out his commands. Many Old Testament passages suggest that he responds with wrath or anger when people disobey his commands. Perhaps there are situations in which he reacts with anger to one's failure to carry out his expectations (that are not at the same time commands), but disappointment seems to be the more likely reaction in many other situations.

SIN, EXPECTATION, AND ACTS THAT ARE DISCOURAGED

Is it always sinful to perform actions that God discourages? Is it always sinful to fail to do what God expects one to do or to do what God expects one to refrain from doing? It seems unlikely that both of these questions are to be answered in the affirmative.

Is it sometimes sinful to perform actions that God discourages but does not forbid? Is it sometimes sinful to fail to do what God expects but does not require one to do or to do what God expects but does not require one to refrain from doing? It seems likely that that both of these questions are to be answered in the affirmative.

Therefore, it seems likely that sometimes but not always it is sinful to do what God discourages but does not forbid. God arguably discourages rudeness, for example, but it is hard to imagine that every conceivable instance of rudeness qualifies as a sin. A person might unknowingly and unintentionally exhibit rudeness while interacting with someone in an unfamiliar culture; I believe that few if any would classify this act of rudeness as a sin. The same might even be true of behavior that is known to be rude, such as asking for a fork in an Asian restaurant after deciding to be a bit rude rather than messy. On the other end of the spectrum, there are no doubt actions of intentional rudeness that are so egregious that they qualify as sinful. In short, some instances of rudeness qualify as sinful and some do not.

Someone might object that an act of rudeness that is so egregious as to qualify as sinful is at the same time forbidden by God, not merely discouraged by him. And if this is true, the objector might continue, there are perhaps no acts of rudeness that are both sinful and not forbidden by God. Similar remarks might involve other actions God discourages: God does not forbid actions he discourages when they are mild enough not to qualify as sinful, but any acts serious enough to qualify as sinful are at the same time forbidden.

It might be helpful to recall from an earlier chapter that Islam recognizes five degrees of sin. The lowest level is comprised of mistakes, the second level of immorality, the third of transgressions, then wickedness and depravity, and finally idolatry. This hierarchy seems to comport well with Islamic ethics. The higher levels of sin tend to fall into the category of the forbidden, and the lower levels tend to fall into the category of the discouraged (some mistakes might even be classified as permitted). Surely, therefore, it is likely that at least some sins are discouraged but not forbidden.

Of course, this does not completely settle the matter. One might continue to insist that there is no common ground between what counts as a sin and what God discourages without forbidding it. One motivation for holding this view, as stated earlier, is the view that no sin whatsoever escapes God's censure and is therefore forbidden. But a different motivation for holding this view is that some sins are so inconsequential that they fall into the category of the permitted, while those that are consequential fall into the category of the forbidden, with nothing left in between.

At the end of the day I must admit that, although I find both of these views highly implausible, I do not have a foolproof response to either. Perhaps the situation of the moral landscape can be pictured in Boolean terms. The category of sin certainly overlaps with the category of what God forbids, and the category of what God forbids certainly overlaps with the category of what God discourages. All sides can agree with these claims. The key question is whether there is any overlap between the category of sin and the category of what God discourages such that this area of overlap lies outside the category of what God forbids, and I believe this is likely. Along the spectrum of rude acts ranging from the unintentional to the egregious, I believe it is likely that some in the middle range qualify as sins that God discourages but does not forbid.

I close this chapter with two possible examples: squirting water from a hose at a neighbor's obnoxious barking poodle and using profanity in a gathering of pious church members in an effort to produce shock and outrage. Naturally the objector who is convinced that no sin is at the same time discouraged but not forbidden by God will not be persuaded by these examples. And those sympathetic to my point of view might also not be persuaded by my examples, believing that better examples can be found. Perhaps they are right. I do not wish my point of view to rise or fall on the strength of the examples I have provided.

CHAPTER SEVEN

MORAL IDEALS, VIRTUE ETHICS, AND SIN

The sinful actions of human beings are sometimes thought of in terms of the failure to achieve that which is ideal. In an ideal world, according to this way of thinking, there would be no sin. Recall from chapter 2 Plantinga's assertion that sin interferes with the way things are supposed to be. Since the way things are supposed to be expresses an ideal, sin can be thought of as something that interferes with an ideal order.

In this chapter I will examine one type of ideal, the type that operates in the moral domain. I will argue that there is not just one moral ideal but a multiplicity of moral ideals. But what exactly is a moral ideal? Many philosophers have spoken of moral ideals, but seldom have they offered a definition or formal account of a moral ideal. In an effort to clarify what exactly is meant by a moral ideal, I will devote the first section of this chapter to arriving at a precise account of what it is. In the second section I will describe what I take to be the relationship between moral ideals and moral virtues: practicing a moral virtue is a key factor in attaining or achieving a moral ideal. In the third section I will explain the manner in which sin enters the picture. Sin can take the form of failing to achieve a certain type of moral ideal. In addition, sin can take the form of failure to develop moral virtue, an intention to develop moral vice, or simply the practice of moral vice.

MORAL IDEALS

At a young age, Agnes Gonxha Bojaxhiu, whom we know as Mother Teresa, was fascinated with the work of missionaries in Bengal. Over time this and other early experiences helped produce in her a growing sense of compassion for the poor and underprivileged. At some point compassion began to function as a moral ideal in her outlook on the world, and it remained so for the rest of her life.

Since the time of Plato, philosophers have talked about moral ideals, but seldom have they attempted to offer a formal definition of "moral ideals" or even to describe in more than a sentence or two what they are. What exactly are moral ideals, and how exactly do they relate to other moral concepts? Where in the moral landscape can they be found, and how do they function in the lives of moral agents? How should we characterize the contrast between moral ideals and non-moral ideals?

I do not pretend to have answers to all of these questions, but I will make a preliminary inquiry into the nature of moral ideals in a way that may provide at least partial answers to these questions. In the first section of this chapter I will look at what a number of philosophers have to say about moral ideals. In the second section I will contend that moral ideals occupy a space in the moral terrain close to that of moral virtues. The discussion will be limited to the possession of moral ideals by human persons; some, like Charles Taylor (2007), have talked about authenticity as a moral ideal possessed by entire cultures.

The account I provisionally adopt is constructed of insights from William Frankena, John Hare, and Robert Audi. A promising place to begin, I believe, is with Frankena's characterization of having moral ideals: "Having a moral ideal is wanting to be a person of a given sort, having certain traits of character rather than others, for example, moral courage or perfect integrity" (Frankena 1963, 54). Frankena is not telling us directly what moral ideals are; he is telling us what it means to have a moral ideal. What it means to have a moral ideal, he says, is wanting to be a certain kind of person, a person with certain traits of character.

Let us proceed with the idea that having a moral ideal is to have certain traits of character, traits such as moral courage or perfect integrity

(Frankena's examples). Perhaps Frankena's view is that moral ideals simply are traits of character. After all, if having X is identical to having Y, it is hard to resist the conclusion that X is identical to Y. If this was Frankena's view, having a moral ideal certainly is the same thing as having certain traits of character. Whether this was his view is not entirely certain. Nevertheless, I find it plausible to judge that in his view moral ideals simply are envisioned traits of character.

Another option, if we were to follow Plato's lead, would be to hold that moral ideals are Platonic ideals of a certain sort. We might think of courage as something that lies outside all of us as we strive to realize it in our day-to-day lives. I do not have a knock-down refutation of this view, but I believe that Frankena's approach has at least two advantages over it. First, thinking of moral ideals as traits of character does not commit one to the existence of dubious universals. This is not to say that universals are objectionable in and of themselves. Acknowledging the property of having courage does not seem objectionable, but one might well question whether such a thing as the Platonic form of courage exists.

Second, construing moral ideals as traits of character makes it easier to provide an account of the motivational force of these ideals. If moral ideals are ideals of the Platonic sort, an account is needed as to how they become internalized to the point of motivating behavior (DeMarco 1995, 207), whereas if moral ideals are traits of character, a motivational account seems relatively straightforward and one can envision moral ideals as having a strong moral grip on one. I do not take these to be decisive considerations, but perhaps they are enough to tip the balance in the direction of Frankena's account. Because I know of no contemporary philosophers (as opposed to historical figures) who hold this view about moral ideals, I will say no more about them.

Aristotle's discussion of kind-specific attributions of excellence may well provide the inspiration for what R. M. Hare says about moral ideals: "To have an ideal . . . is to think of some kind of thing as pre-eminently good within some larger class. . . . To have a moral ideal is to think of some type of man as a pre-eminently good type of man, or, possibly, of some type of society as a preeminently good one" (Hare 1969, 159). If we think of a moral ideal in terms of a preeminently good type of man or woman, we are left with an account that squares with Frankena's account, provided that a good type of man is a man with good character traits. I am not certain whether Hare's intent was to think of moral ideals in quite this fashion, but it seems safe to say that his account is compatible with Frankena's. Thus we can adopt the terminology of "pre-eminently good" in arriving at the view that moral ideals are character traits of a pre-eminently good variety.

Bernard Gert does not propose a definition of "moral ideals," but according to him, acting on a moral ideal is "intentionally acting so as to avoid, prevent, or relieve the suffering of harm by someone protected by the moral system" (Gert 2004, 22). In his view people are only encouraged, not required, to follow moral ideals. That we are not required to follow them is a view shared by Frankena (1963) and Tom Beauchamp (1995), who appear to hold that following moral ideals is supererogatory. Hence they agree with Gert that we are at most encouraged to follow them. Sidgwick speaks of moral ideals as being "attractive rather than imperative" (Sidgwick 1981, 105), and his view also seems to agree with Gert's position.

The question of whether or not moral ideals are required of us has been taken up by Robert Audi (2005), who has called into question the view that we are not required to follow moral ideals. He argues that at times we are obliged to follow moral ideals, contending that veracity and sincerity are moral ideals that we are obliged to pursue. It is not entirely optional for us to follow these ideals; at least this is not the case all of the time. On certain occasions we are required to pursue the moral ideal of veracity, and on certain other occasions we are required to pursue the moral ideal of sincerity. Hence Audi takes issue with the position of Gert, Frankena, and Beauchamp, who believe it is never obligatory to pursue moral ideals.

Some philosophers have defended the opposite position, that it is always obligatory to pursue moral ideals (or at least certain moral ideals). Utilitarians such as Brandt (1971) and Slote (1992) identify ideals that they believe we have an ongoing moral duty to bring about (I take bringing about a moral ideal to be even stronger than pursuing a moral ideal, which I take to be attempting to bring about or attain a moral ideal). Elizabeth Pybus (1982) argues on prescriptivist grounds that we have a moral duty to pursue moral ideals. And Immanuel Kant held the position that pursuing moral ideals can be nothing other than a duty (see the opening sentences of *Religion within the Limits of Reason*, Book II, Section 1).

Audi's position strikes me as a sensible middle path. At times we have moral obligations to pursue or even attain moral ideals. At other times, pursuing or attaining a moral ideal is optional from a moral point of view. And sometimes, when it is optional, pursuing or attaining a moral ideal can be supererogatory.

In the remainder of this chapter I will follow Frankena in regarding moral ideals as traits of character, I will follow Hare in regarding these traits of character as preeminently good, and I will follow Audi in regarding moral ideals as optional at some times and obligatory at other times. To say that a person has a particular moral ideal is at least to say that he or she is a preeminently good person when it comes to exemplifying or manifesting the trait of that moral ideal.

MORAL IDEALS AND MORAL VIRTUES

I turn now to the relationship between moral ideals and moral virtues. I will assume that the Aristotelian tradition is correct in identifying moral virtues as dispositions to act in a certain way.[1] If moral virtues are indeed dispositions to act in a certain way, how do they relate to moral ideals?

Some might be tempted to believe that moral ideals are identical to moral virtues. One reason this view might be tempting is that the same term, such as "courage," can be used to refer to a moral ideal and to a moral virtue. But I believe this temptation should be resisted. If we follow Frankena in regarding moral ideals as traits of character, as I propose to do, the view under consideration yields the conclusion that traits of character are nothing more than dispositions to act. Some might be willing to bite the bullet and grant the conclusion that traits of character are nothing more than dispositions to act (a view that may be a species of behaviorism). I will remain open to the possibility that this conclusion is correct. But in the remainder of this chapter I will proceed on the assumption that some traits of character are not identical to dispositions (certainly bad character traits are not identical to moral virtues, and the same is true of character traits that are not of a moral nature).

What distinguishes these moral ideals from mere dispositions to act? If these character traits are preeminently good, the answer would appear to be that the dispositions to act are accompanied by a conscious desire to thereby realize good. Suppose that I have achieved the virtue of justice and I am thereby disposed to perform acts of justice as opportunities arise in my life. As I perform these acts of justice I need not perform them with a conscious desire to bring about good. But if justice functions in my life as a moral ideal, a preeminently good character trait, I will presumably perform these acts of justice with a conscious desire to bring about good. This might take the form of desiring that those who benefit from these acts of justice will thereby flourish.

If Frankena is correct in holding that moral ideals are character traits, moral ideals would appear to be closely related to moral virtues. Thus the moral virtue of courage is closely related to the moral ideal of courage. I suggest that they are related in the following way: Practicing the moral virtue of courage increases the likelihood of attaining the character trait of courage. In this way moral virtue contributes to the attainment of moral ideals. A strategy for the acquisition of a moral ideal is practicing the moral virtue associated with it.

This is a point worth stressing in terms of developing moral ideals. Developing a particular character trait might strike one as a stiff challenge. But if the development of moral virtue can be seen as a strategy for developing a character trait, the challenge becomes more manageable. Aristotle's great insight concerning moral virtue was that practicing virtue is the key to attaining it. One who performs just actions over a period of time eventually performs them out of habit and thereby attains the moral virtue of justice. And my suggestion is that attaining the virtue of justice makes the acquisition of justice as a character trait more likely. This is not to say that one who has attained the virtue of justice will inevitably develop a conscious desire to bring about good, but one who has already developed a conscious desire to bring about justice seems a likely candidate to develop a conscious desire to bring about good.

Julia Annas believes that "virtues are dispositions which are not only admirable but which we find *inspiring* and take as *ideals* to aspire to, precisely because of the commitment to goodness which they embody" (Annas 2011, 109). I believe this statement is compatible with my account.

Suppose that I find the virtue of courage to be inspiring and take it as an ideal to aspire to. Surely this can take the form of wishing to develop courage as a character trait, and one way to accomplish this is to practice the virtue of courage.

So far my examples have been restricted to moral virtues and character traits that have identical labels. The beauty of the approach under consideration is that strategies of a variegated nature are also possible. The development of a particular character trait might be promoted by the development of each of several distinct moral virtues together with the avoidance of certain vices. For example, someone who wishes to develop the moral ideal of diligence might do so by practicing the virtues of perseverance, industry, and assiduity and striving to avoid the vices of lethargy, indolence, and procrastination.

All of this is not to say that the only way to develop moral ideals is by developing moral virtues. Presumably one's early moral education will be a more decisive factor in shaping one's character traits. But assuming that it is possible to acquire in adulthood moral ideals that one does not already possess, one can take advantage of the close relationship between character traits and moral virtues. One can practice a moral virtue as a strategy toward the development of an associated character trait.

Perhaps the acquisition of moral ideals is not an all-or-nothing affair. Suppose that someone is in the process of acquiring a character trait but has not yet fully acquired it. Can this partially acquired character trait function as a moral ideal for this person in a less-than-complete manner? I see no reason why not. A moral ideal's mode of operation in a person's life is something that admits of degrees. Compassion functioned as a moral ideal in the life of Mother Teresa, and yet it is possible that as a young woman it functioned in her life in a less-than-complete manner.

MORAL IDEALS, MORAL VIRTUE, AND SIN

I turn now to discussing the relevance of the foregoing discussion to the practice of sin. The first thesis I shall put forward is that the avoidance of sin can qualify as a moral ideal. The reason is that the avoidance of sin can function as a character trait, indeed one that some religious traditions endeavor to instill in young persons. Moreover, it is possible for one to be preeminently good in manifesting this character trait. Therefore, in terms of the moral ideals adopted in the first section of this chapter, the avoidance of sin can qualify as a moral ideal.

In addition, the avoidance of a particular type of sin can qualify as a moral ideal. For example, recall that according to Audi, veracity is a moral ideal, from which it follows that veracity is a character trait that one might manifest. To the extent that one manifests it, one avoids the sin of lying. Hence one can identify the moral ideal of veracity as the moral ideal of the avoidance of the sin of lying. No doubt there are other moral ideals that can be identified as the avoidance of a particular category of sin.

One might feel that these observations are not particularly helpful and do not succeed in shedding much light on escaping from sin and its attractions. More helpful perhaps would be to concentrate on the close relationship between moral ideals and moral virtues. Recall that the practice of moral virtue contributes significantly to attaining moral ideals. Just as the avoidance of sin can qualify as a moral ideal, the avoidance of sin can qualify as a moral virtue that contributes to attaining such an ideal. And just as the avoidance of sin can qualify as a moral virtue, the failure to develop moral virtue can qualify as a sin, at least when it is deliberate.

Suppose that someone has been taught the importance of practicing the virtue of justice as a means of becoming a just individual. In a spirit of rebellion, this person decides to have no part in this process, having been convinced by Glaucon in Plato's *Republic* that practicing injustice brings more happiness than practicing justice. This person, in addition, desires to withhold benefits from others as far as possible, and this also plays a part in his wish to avoid practicing justice. I believe that something is seriously wrong with this person's approach to the virtue of justice, and regarding it as sinful (to at least a modest degree) seems quite plausible.

There are occasions, therefore, in which the failure to develop a moral virtue can qualify as sinful. Not everyone might agree that the example I have provided is an instance of this phenomenon, but it is hard to deny that the deliberate failure to develop moral virtue is sometimes sinful to at least a modest degree.

Consider next the intent to develop a moral vice. If intentions can be sinful, as seems reasonable, the intent to develop a moral vice is a prime candidate for an intent that qualifies as sinful. Suppose that a person decides that he wishes to develop the vice of cruelty and forms the intention to develop this vice. His intention is to inflict cruelty on others, including animals, whenever the opportunity presents itself. Judging that this intention is sinful to at least a modest degree strikes me as uncontroversial.

Finally, the practice of a moral vice can be sinful. The practice of a moral vice is probably a paradigmatic example of what is sinful, depending on the vice. If lethargy is a moral vice—and some may doubt whether it is—practicing it will ordinarily not be sinful. On the other hand, it will ordinarily be sinful to practice racism. I conclude that the failure to develop moral virtue can, under certain circumstances, be sinful, as can the intent to develop a moral vice and the practice of a moral vice. I do not pretend to have plumbed the depths of explaining the relationship among moral virtue, moral vice, and sin, but I believe one can reasonably agree with the claims I have put forward. More will be said in the next chapter regarding the relationship between the practice of moral vice and sin.

The moral life has a richness and complexity that is not always made evident in discussions about ethics. Carrying out one's moral duties and living in accord with one's moral responsibilities are of primary concern. In addition, a concern for the aretaic dimensions of morality leads one to practice moral virtue and avoid moral vice. But this is not the whole story. Philosophers such as Frankena, Gert, Audi, and Hare have recognized that moral ideals are also an important part of the moral life. I have endeavored to argue that moral ideals cannot be reduced to the aretaic, but they are nevertheless intertwined in a way that has the potential to give us a deeper understanding of sin and its avoidance. I hope to have suggested some ways in which such an understanding can come about.

CHAPTER EIGHT

SIN AND SYMBOLISM

The symbolism of sin is a familiar notion. The color red is sometimes said to symbolize sin (as in Isaiah 1:18, "Though your sins be as scarlet . . . "), and symbolism of this type can in some ways enhance our understanding of sin. However, in this chapter I will present a concept of symbolism derived from the work of Robert Nozick that will allow us to understand the symbolism of sin on a deeper level.

The first section of this chapter will present Nozick's notion of symbolic value and explain how it contributes to our understanding of virtue ethics. The second section illustrates the application of this notion to sin or, more specifically, sins that take the form of acts of vice. The final section broadens the discussion to the consideration of group behavior.

SYMBOLIC VALUE

In his book *The Nature of Rationality*, Robert Nozick introduces the notion of the symbolic utility of an act (Nozick 1993, 26ff). Although much has been written about symbolism and symbolic meaning, Nozick breaks important new ground in showing how the moral status of an act can be affected by that which is symbolized by the performance of an act (or by the process of this symbolization). His work is significant, in large part, because it brings together two areas of philosophy, ethics and the philosophy of language, in a manner that has strong potential for shedding light on both areas. In this section I attempt to describe and clarify the main features of his theory, to discuss some applications of it, and to do so in such a way as to highlight the interplay that is created between these two areas.

Since the concept of utility is the focal point of Nozick's discussion, what he says about symbolic utility has a decidedly consequentialist emphasis. I hope to show that the concept of symbolic utility can be useful in understanding other areas of morality, such as virtue ethics, and that it is particularly useful in illuminating acts of virtue or vice in group settings. Because the term "utility" carries with it strong consequentialist connotations, I shall employ the more neutral terminology of the "symbolic value" of an act throughout the remainder of the discussion.

The basic idea of the symbolic value of an act is relatively straightforward: The performance of one act can symbolize the performance of other actual or potential acts or states of affairs in a manner that has moral significance. Roughly speaking, moral value, whether positive or negative, is produced as the result of the symbolization. As Nozick puts it, value "flows back" along symbolic (as opposed to causal) lines from the future acts in the series to the original act (Nozick 1993, 27). Thus the notion of symbolic value as articulated here is considerably narrower than the relation of ordinary symbolization. Communicating to a deaf person through the use of sign language involves performing acts that symbolize various states of affairs. But these states of affairs would ordinarily not qualify as the symbolic value of the acts that are performed, for no moral dimension as such is built into the practice of communicating through sign language. Thus it is Nozick's key insight that the linguistic concept of symbolization has a rich moral component, one that has been explored neither by philosophers of language nor by moral philosophers.

A simple example of symbolic value can be seen in the practice of promising. Making a promise symbolizes the future act of carrying out the promise (and this is so regardless of whether the promise is actually carried out). Another simple example is raising one's hand when volunteers are being solicited to perform a particular task. This action symbolizes the future act of performing the task. In each of these examples there is an implicit moral dimension: If one breaks one's promises, one is morally blameworthy, and if one volunteers one is morally praiseworthy, but if one volunteers and does not follow through, one is morally blameworthy.

Promising and volunteering are actions whose symbolic value depends on the presence of certain conventions. Because certain conventions are in place, people who make promises or volunteer for certain activities are expected to follow through. Sometimes the presence of these conventions confers on otherwise mundane acts a high degree of significance, as in the case of the symbolic value created by placing a ring on another's finger when it occurs in the context of a wedding ceremony or the symbolic value created by acts performed in the context of religious ceremonies.

However, it is important to recognize that symbolic value can likewise be conferred in the absence of conventions. In general, there are two kinds of symbolism, symbolism that depends on the presence of conventions and symbolism that does not. When one's small child performs an act of generosity, the symbolic value can consist in its symbolizing a pattern of acts of generosity extending into the future. The act of generosity simply represents actions of a similar sort, and the child's parents can derive great satisfaction as the result of this representation. But it is not because it falls within the context of certain conventions that this representation takes place; it takes place because one act can stand for or symbolize other acts that are relevantly similar.

The symbolic value of an act is not normally the same as a disposition to act. If I volunteer to perform a task, my act of volunteering may signify a willingness to perform the task (and it may also signify a willingness to volunteer for tasks). However, what is signified by an act is not in general identical to the symbolic value of an act. There may be special cases in which the symbolic value consists (at least in part) of dispositions to act, as when I promise to be willing to do something. But the disposition signified by an act is not necessarily its symbolic value.

Part of what determines the symbolic value of an act is the agent's intent in performing the act, but it is also determined in part by the perception of the act by others. Suppose that a man who has been convicted of a heinous crime is sentenced by a judge to merely twenty hours of community service. Because the public perception is that the judge has been far too lenient, the act may serve to symbolize future ludicrously lenient sentences to other convicted criminals. But this symbolic value need not reflect the intent of the judge, for the judge may have no intent to issue lenient sentences in the future.

One of the central contentions of the present discussion is that the notion of symbolic value can lead to a better understanding of virtue ethics. When a person performs a single act of virtue, this act can symbolize or stand for other potential acts of the virtue in question. For that matter, it can symbolize acts of other virtues, but here I will concentrate on virtues or vices one at a time. According to an Aristotelian account of moral virtue, an agent can acquire a moral virtue, in part, by practicing the virtue—that is, by performing a series of acts that exemplify the virtue. And it could be said of one particular act in this series that it symbolizes the performance of the others in this series. When a just person performs a just act, this act can symbolize a lifetime of just acts performed by this person.

But not all acts of justice are performed by just persons or even by persons who are on their way to becoming just persons, and it is here that Nozick's ideas begin to be helpful. When a person performs a single just act, this act can symbolize the potential performance of other just acts. And it is crucial to emphasize that these potential performances need not be actual performances. Whether or not the person ever performs another just act, the performance of this just act symbolizes the performance of other potential just acts by the same person. Part of what is gratifying about a single act of virtue is that it symbolizes something larger than itself, the possibility of additional future acts of the virtue by the same person. The symbolic value of the act encourages us to think in terms of a pattern extending into the future, and we can think in terms of this pattern whether or not it actually occurs.

SYMBOLIC VALUE AND SINS OF VICE

In this section I will assume that actions of vice can be sinful or, in other words, sins can take the form of actions of vice.[1] And just as a single act of virtue can symbolize a pattern of acts of this particular virtue extending into the future, the same is true of vice. A single sinful act of vice can symbolize a pattern of acts of this particular vice extending into the future. A single sinful act of rudeness, for example, can symbolize a pattern of rude actions by the person performing it. Depending on the circumstances, this can be a cause of concern or even alarm. But the potential acts of rudeness that are symbolized by the sinful act of rudeness need not ever actually be performed.

The picture becomes more complicated when the concept of symbolic value is applied to series of acts performed by more then one agent. The performance of an act of virtue or vice can, I suggest, symbolize additional acts of the same virtue or vice by several agents. To take a simple example, one that does not constitute a sinful act, we criticize someone's throwing a gum wrapper on an otherwise immaculate park lawn. If the person is a chronic litterer, our criticism may be rooted in the act's proceeding from a fixed and unchangeable disposition, to use Aristotelian terminology. But if the person is not a habitual litterer, nor thought to be one, we must look in a different direction for the source of our moral displeasure. I suggest that the act of throwing down a gum wrapper symbolizes a series of similar acts by a variety of people, with the end result that the park becomes filled with litter. In like manner, a sinful act by one person can symbolize a series of sinful acts by multiple people. The act is viewed as part of a possible or potential pattern based not on a series of acts by one individual but on a series of acts by many individuals.

Discussions of virtue ethics sometimes focus on the virtue or vice of individual moral agents and leave the impression that virtue or vice is something that characterizes only the behavior patterns of individuals. But there is a growing recognition among philosophical ethicists that virtue ethics has a communitarian dimension as well. Alasdair MacIntyre, for example, states, "I am never able to seek for the good or exercise the virtues only *qua* individual" (MacIntyre 1981, 204). And although those who advocate a communitarian approach to virtue ethics do not explicitly address the question of whether virtue and vice can be meaningfully ascribed to a series of acts by a variety of moral agents, this possibility clearly seems in keeping with this communitarian spirit.

The possibility of ascribing virtue or vice to a series of acts by more than one moral agent, moreover, is a phenomenon that seems to be recognized in ordinary discourse. When someone claims to have been treated rudely by the clerks in a certain store, it is natural to interpret this claim as ascribing rudeness to a pattern of acts by different clerks. Just as we take note of a pattern of rude acts by one individual over time, we sometimes take note of a pattern of rude acts by various agents. The notion of symbolic value accommodates this intuition. It allows for the possibility of speaking about a virtuous or vicious pattern of behavior involving more than one moral agent, and it allows us to see a connection between a single act of virtue by one moral agent and a pattern of virtuous acts by many moral agents.

An act of virtue or vice not only can symbolize a virtuous or vicious pattern of behavior by several agents but can also, by extension, symbolize a foreseeable outcome produced by this pattern. Thus the single act of littering not only symbolizes a potential pattern of littering but also conjures up images of a park with great quantities of litter.

An awareness of this phenomenon can shed some light on the practice described in chapter 2 as scapegoating. When something unfortunate or inconvenient happens, there is sometimes a tendency to single out someone as the scapegoat for this state of affairs. Perhaps a sinful act of vice by this person can be identified as tangentially related to the unfortunate event and condemnation of this act of vice provides a way for people to vent their rage and frustration when other factors leading to the unfortunate event are not known. This sinful act of vice symbolizes similar acts of vice by other unknown individuals, and it ultimately symbolizes the unfortunate state of affairs that results.

There is something manifestly unfair about the practice of scapegoating, and a case could be made that scapegoating itself qualifies as sinful. But the point of the present discussion is that the practice of scapegoating is built on recognizing the symbolic value of an act of vice. We focus on a single sinful act of vice, and this act symbolizes other actions of vice by the same person or different persons and ultimately the unwanted outcome. Several years ago in Michigan, a longtime member of the state legislature was observed illegally parking in a space designated as for the handicapped. The incident was reported by the press, a great deal of negative sentiment was directed by the public toward this individual, and in the very next election he lost to a little-known challenger. There are many people who park illegally in spaces designated as for the handicapped, and this deplorable state of affairs can be a source of rage and frustration to the general public. Thus, when a prominent member of the community was identified as parking in such a space, it created an opportunity for people to vent their rage or frustration.

Again, selecting one person as the scapegoat seems unjust. Yet it is remarkable how frequently this practice occurs, and not only among ordinary individuals. Political leaders, journalists, trial attorneys, and other professionals engage in this practice in one form or another with regularity. Sometimes people even target themselves when it becomes apparent that others will inevitably do so. Arriving at a full understanding as to why this practice is so deeply entrenched in our present culture—why it is so widespread and why so much credence is given to those who practice it— is perhaps difficult. However, at least part of the answer lies in the concept of symbolic value. As long as a sinful act of vice by one person comes to symbolize a troublesome situation, people will find it convenient to criticize this particular act. Once again, Nozick's model enables us to deepen our understanding of a phenomenon from the moral sphere by applying tools developed in the sphere of language.

The opposite practice, singling out someone as the object of praise for a beneficial state of affairs when the person's act of virtue is only tangentially connected to the outcome as a whole, seems to occur less frequently. But this situation can likewise be characterized in terms of symbolic value. People focus on a single act of virtue and allow it to symbolize other unknown acts of virtue. When many survivors are rescued at the scene of a disaster, one of the rescuers may emerge as a hero because his or her act of virtue happens to be captured by a press photographer. The heroism of this rescuer comes to symbolize the heroism of many rescuers and the successful rescue itself, and it thereby provides the focal point for the feelings of gratitude that are experienced.

SYMBOLIC VALUE, SIN, AND THE BEHAVIOR OF GROUPS

Symbolic value is also helpful in understanding some of the dynamics of groups or collectives. Sometimes questions arise about the extent to which the actions of one member affect the moral status of other members of a collective. Suppose that a certain club is committed to an ideology of racism and one of its members performs a sinful act of racism. Some moralists would be inclined to say that all of the club's members share moral responsibility or bear collective responsibility for this act of vice or for its effects. Others, of a more individualist persuasion, will feel that this is too severe a view and that it is unfair to ascribe the responsibility for the act or its effects to the other members. But, although it is difficult to settle disputes about group responsibility, all sides can agree that the sinful act of racism is at least symbolic of potential acts of racism by the other members. It is in this sense that the single sinful act of racism reflects on the other members, even though they may never have actually performed an act of racism. Thus, even if one does not come to bear moral responsibility for what another member of one's group has done, one is linked to the actions of the other by membership in the group.

As discussed in chapter 2, people sometimes claim to experience collective guilt for a sinful act of vice committed by one or more of the members of a group or collective. On a superficial level it may seem irrational to experience guilt for what another has done. But here, too, the notion of symbolic value is helpful: If this member's sinful act of vice is genuinely symbolic of what the other members might do, it may be perfectly reasonable to feel a certain type of guilt for the sinful act. If a fellow member of one's group commits a sinful act of racism, feelings of collective guilt by other members may be quite reasonable. And part of what makes these feelings reasonable or understandable is the symbolic value of the act. If one thinks strictly in terms of causal connections, the notion of collective guilt can seem to make little sense (after all, how can an agent bear guilt for something he or she did not in any sense bring about?). But if one recognizes the value that flows back along symbolic lines, an entirely different perspective on collective guilt emerges.

Whether feelings of collective guilt are reasonable or understandable depends largely on the nature of the collective. In the example under consideration, the members of the collective are linked by a common ideology of racism. Feelings of collective guilt are definitely more understandable in this context than they would be in the absence of this common ideology (though the members committed to an ideology of racism may be less susceptible to feelings of guilt over the racist act of a fellow member in the first place). A sinful act of racism definitely reflects on fellow members with more intensity if they have joined a club professing an ideology of racism. On the other hand, feelings of collective guilt would rarely have a rational basis in a collective with a more or less random composition, such as the passengers in a subway car.

There is another way in which symbolic value is operative in the performance of an act of virtue or vice by a member of a collective. Elsewhere (Mellema 1998, 133ff) I have argued that a collective is morally responsible for a state of affairs only if each member of the collective performs a contributing act, an act by virtue of whose performance he or she comes to have membership in the collective. According to this view, one must actually do something or omit doing something to be part of a group that is collectively responsible for an outcome (although one is not necessarily rendered morally responsible as an individual for this outcome by one's contributing act). Thus collective responsibility is not like a virus that infects people who come into contact with it. Membership in the collective depends on the performance of an act or the omission of an act.

Not everyone may agree with this account of collective responsibility, but suppose, for the sake of argument, that it is correct. In such a case, if the members of the club committed to an ideology of racism are collectively responsible for the outcome of the racist act committed by one of its members, the contributing act of each member could be identified as the act of vice that consists in joining the club. Because someone has joined the club, this person is part of the collective that bears moral responsibility for the outcome of the racist act. Symbolic value can now be seen to be operative on two different levels. First, the act of racism symbolizes potential acts of racism by the other members. Second, each member's contributing act symbolizes potential acts of racism. The very act of joining a club committed to an ideology of racism symbolizes one's future potential racist behavior.

This is not to say that one's joining the club demonstrates a commitment to future acts of racism or even a propensity or readiness to commit such acts. But there is definitely something symbolic in one's joining a club committed to racism (in addition to being offensive in and of itself), and part of what it seems to symbolize is one's capability to act in a racist manner, or at least one's having a condoning attitude toward performing such acts. Perhaps it is conceivable for a person to be committed to racism only at the level of ideology and never on the level of overt action, and hence it is conceivable that a person joining this club may be opposed to actually performing sinful acts of racism. But even if cases such as this are possible, they do not prove that the agent's joining the club cannot symbolize his or her performing future potential acts of racism. The symbolic value of an act is determined in part by the intentions of the agent performing the act, but other factors, such as the message conveyed to others by the act, are also relevant.

As seen in earlier chapters, Anthony Appiah and others have argued that moral agents can be tainted by the evil acts of others with whom they are connected in some significant manner. One who is tainted by such acts does not bear moral responsibility or belong to a collective that bears moral responsibility for these acts or their consequences, but Appiah argues that one's moral integrity is nevertheless affected. Thus a man can be tainted by the criminal acts of his brother, and a surgical nurse can be tainted by the medical malpractice of a physician whom he or she assists. While it may be false to judge that the man bears responsibility for his brother's criminal acts or that the nurse bears moral responsibility for the physician's malpractice, Appiah's point is that their moral integrity is nevertheless adversely affected.

Here it is not my purpose to comment on whether or not there is such a moral category as taint. But if there is such a moral category, it is plausible to suppose that the concept of symbolic value can help explain the basis for ascribing moral taint. For example, imagine a society with a tyrannical dictator. One day a common citizen is overheard making disparaging comments about him. The dictator is so angry that not only is the citizen thrown into prison, but so are all of his brothers as well. While one can certainly raise questions about the fairness of imprisoning the innocent brothers, the point of the present discussion is that if they are tainted by the sin of their brother, it is in part because his sin symbolizes their doing the same. Although none of them defamed the dictator, their brother's doing so is symbolic of their having done so as well. In general, tainting can take place when the act of an evildoer symbolizes a similar act by one to whom this person is connected in some significant manner.

Paul Ricoeur describes essentially this same phenomenon in a discussion of defilement. According to him, defilement is a symbol of evil: "Defilement is to stain or spot what lustration is to washing. . . . It is a symbolic stain" (Ricoeur 1967, 36). If I am defiled by the stain that attaches to my criminal brother, it is by virtue of symbolization that this takes place. The defilement that attaches to me is a symbolic stain; it is symbolic of the stain that attaches to him.

When the collective is a formal organization, such as a corporation, with established hierarchies of authority, the symbolic value of an act of virtue or vice can be striking in its effect on the thinking of those both inside and outside the organization. The symbolic value of actions by people in positions of corporate leadership is likely to take on exaggerated significance. When corporate leaders perform acts of virtue while acting in an official capacity, these acts symbolize virtuous patterns of acts throughout the organization. Those within the organization are likely to be inspired to perform acts of virtue, and those outside the organization are likely to form impressions of the organization as a place where the virtue in question is likely to be practiced. Similar remarks apply to sinful acts of vice performed by corporate leaders acting in an official capacity.

Those who write about business ethics frequently talk about the importance of promoting a favorable moral climate in an organization, and I believe it is helpful to see that the moral climate is determined, at least in part, by the symbolic value of these acts of virtue and vice. Those in positions of leadership are frequently said to set the moral tone of an organization, and what this means is that the acts of virtue or vice performed by these people are highly symbolic of a wider pattern of virtue or vice. The moral climate is constitutive of this wider pattern, and for this reason it is important for those in positions of leadership to consider the symbolic value of what they do when they act in the name of the organization. Traditional ethical theories have stressed the importance of acting out of good will or bringing about good consequences. But it is important, especially for public figures, to ascertain something else as well, namely, what their actions symbolize. And part of what this involves is ascertaining how these acts appear in the eyes of others.

While the symbolic value of the actions of these public figures can take on significance, it is also worth pointing out that their inaction can have significant symbolic value. Suppose that a senior-level manager in a large corporation receives a report from a subordinate describing a decision he or she has made, and suppose that the action being described is highly questionable in terms of good ethics. The manager can exercise veto power over the action but elects not to, and the decision is implemented. Here the symbolic value of the manager's inaction can be significant. It can encourage subordinates to take questionable courses of action in the future, and to others it may symbolize the willingness of the firm's leadership to overlook or condone questionable decisions in the firm.

The same phenomenon can be observed in governmental decision making. Just as the symbolic value of action or inaction by influential persons in corporations can take on an exaggerated significance, the same is sometimes true of actions of virtue or vice performed by governmental authorities. Nozick speaks of an example in which a decision is made about whether to save a trapped miner. The symbolic value of a negative decision on the part of governmental officials for reasons of cost can be chilling in its effects. Only slightly less chilling would be the symbolic value of their taking no action at all. Clearly, public officials would do well to develop an awareness of symbolic value and to take it into account when deciding on courses of action with some measure of visibility.

If it is possible for groups or collectives to perform actions, it is possible to suppose that the actions of groups or collectives can have symbolic value. In formal organizations, work is frequently performed by committees of an organization's personnel. And when a decision is made by a committee, we can speak of the symbolic value of this decision. For example, the symbolic value of a committee's deciding to recommend marketing a product overseas that cannot legally be marketed locally because of suspected health hazards can be significant.

It might be argued that the committee's decision is nothing more than the net effect of several decisions on the part of several different members of the committee. Whether or not group actions can always be analyzed in this fashion is a matter of controversy. But even if such a reduction is possible, it doesn't follow that the symbolic value of a committee decision can be reduced to a composite of the symbolic values of the acts of the committee's component members. The symbolic value of a committee action is determined in part by the appearance it generates among those who are aware of the action, and those who are aware of the action may have no awareness of how the individual committee members contributed to this action. The symbolic value of a committee's decision can, of course, depend to some extent on the symbolic value of its members' actions. This might be the case in situations in which the deliberations of the committee are open to the public and various members of the committee state their reasons for supporting the decision.

CONCLUSION

I have argued that the notion of symbolic value sheds light on some of our moral intuitions regarding acts of virtue and vice. In particular, it sheds light on some of our intuitions regarding acts of vice that are sinful. I have discussed how this takes place in situations involving groups or collectives. The symbolic value of acts performed by persons in positions of leadership can have exaggerated significance, and this is a phenomenon that deserves to be taken more seriously by those who study the ethical dimensions of organizational behavior.

CHAPTER NINE

SIN AND
THE PROBLEM OF EVIL

In David Hume's *Dialogues Concerning Natural Religion* the character named Philo remarks, "Epicurus' old questions are yet unanswered. Is he willing to prevent evil, but not able? Then he is impotent. Is he able but not willing? Then he is malevolent. Is he both able and willing? Whence then is evil?" (Hume 1948, 198).

This chapter is about the so-called problem of evil and its relationship to sin. The first section defines the problem of evil as characterized by philosopher J. L. Mackie. The second section examines the role sin has played in discussions of the problem of evil, most notably in the work of Alvin Plantinga.

In what follows I will assume that a distinction can be drawn between moral evil and natural evil. The philosophical tradition has characterized evil as "whatever is intrinsically bad, bad in itself, or worth avoiding just for its own sake" (Wierenga 2016, 52). So characterized, it is quite evident that some but not all evil is the result of sin. That which is the result of sin is sometimes referred to as moral evil. Natural evil, which includes the suffering caused by natural disasters, is the type of evil that does not result from sinful actions. I will assume, in addition, that a distinction can be drawn between the philosophical problem of evil, the one articulated here by J. L. Mackie, and the pastoral problem of evil. The latter is the result of people's struggling to understand why God allowed horrendous events to occur in their lives. Because they often solicit the advice of pastors in seeking to understand why these events occurred given God's goodness and omnipotence, it is called the pastoral problem of evil. Needless to say, the pastoral problem of evil lies beyond the scope of the present discussion. Also lying beyond the scope of the present discussion is the evidential or probabilistic problem of evil. The problem of evil presented here is known as the deductive problem of evil.

THE DEDUCTIVE PROBLEM OF EVIL

Mackie's account of the problem of evil begins with a consideration of three propositions: (1) God is omnipotent, (2) God is wholly good, and (3) evil exists. He states that there seems to be some contradiction among these three propositions. If God is both omnipotent and wholly good, the existence of evil is quite puzzling. Nevertheless, it is evident that these propositions are not formally contradictory.

Next Mackie introduces two additional propositions that, together with the three original propositions, yield a set of propositions that are formally contradictory. They are: (1) Good is opposed to evil in such a way that a good thing always eliminates evil as far as it can, and (2) there are no limits to what an omnipotent thing can do. In what follows I will refer to the first of these as the elimination principle. Mackie calls these "quasi-logical rules" connecting the terms contained in them. With the addition of these two propositions, Mackie asserts that "a good omnipotent thing eliminates evil completely" (1955, 201).

The dilemma for the theist, then, is that since the two additional propositions are quasi-logical rules and presumably cannot be attacked, one of the original three propositions must be given up on pain of contradiction. Mackie observes that some theists believe that God exists but is less than omnipotent. This concession constitutes what Mackie calls an "adequate solution" and resolves the dilemma by acknowledging the possibility that God is unable to eliminate evil.

Another adequate solution is to hold that evil is an illusion and is therefore not real. Consider the following analogy: Your dog loves to chase cars but cannot do so because he is chained to a large pole. From the dog's lowly perspective, the chain is the greatest evil in the universe, but you realize that the chain is actually something good, not something evil. Perhaps what we as humans consider evil from our lowly perspective is actually not evil at all from God's cosmic perspective. Hence it is entirely possible that evil is an illusion, and if this is so, the theist faces no dilemma in explaining how a good, omnipotent being allows evil.

A different argument to show that evil is not real, one that was sometimes articulated by medieval philosophers, is also built on an analogy. From our knowledge of science we know that cold is nothing more that the absence of heat. Thus cold is no more real in and of itself than the hole of a doughnut. In like manner, evil is nothing more than the absence or privation of good. Like cold, it is nothing real in and of itself, and if evil is not real, there is no need to explain how a good, omnipotent being allows it.

Most theists have resisted Mackie's adequate solutions, refusing to concede that God is less than omnipotent and refusing to acknowledge that all evil is an illusion (the sacred scriptures of some world religions portray evil as something alarmingly real, largely because of sins committed by characters portrayed in these texts).

How, then, should one respond to Mackie and the deductive problem of evil in general? The definitive response by Alvin Plantinga is presented in the next section. But before turning to his "free will defense" I will sketch out some preliminary thoughts. Recall Mackie's elimination principle: Good is opposed to evil in such a way that a good thing always eliminates evil as far as it can. According to Mackie, this is a "quasi-logical rule" connecting the terms it contains, with the implication that one cannot call it into question. But why should we regard this principle as immune from challenge? Isn't it conceivable that a good thing would have reason to allow some evil to exist? Isn't it conceivable that God has reasons to allow some evil to exist?

One could speculate at length what reasons God might have for allowing some evil to exist, but at the end of the day one must admit that God has not revealed these reasons. Nevertheless, it is *possible* that God has reasons for allowing some evil to exist, and if this is true, it is possible that Mackie's elimination principle is false.

Now Mackie is charging that the existence of evil creates a dilemma of a logical nature for the theist who maintains that God is omnipotent and wholly good. For this reason, the burden of proof is on Mackie, who must establish the basis of this dilemma. The elimination principle plays a key role in Mackie's argument, and he provides no defense in support of it. He simply calls it a quasi-logical rule and regards it as obviously true.

Is it obviously true that a good thing always eliminates evil as far as it can? Is it not conceivable that a good thing might, during a certain period of time, have reason to allow at least some evil? Although we might not know God's reasons for allowing evil, is it not possible that God has reasons for allowing some evil? If it is not possible, an explanation is in order as to why it is not possible. Once again, the burden of proof is on Mackie to establish that a wholly good, omnipotent God will of necessity eliminate evil, but he has not done so inasmuch as he has failed to argue on behalf of the elimination principle.

My remarks concerning Mackie have called into question his account of the deductive problem of evil. What I have said about Mackie by no means constitutes an argument that calls into question the deductive problem of evil itself. Others have argued for the deductive problem of evil, and more needs to be said to call into question the deductive problem of evil as such. Plantinga's free will defense is designed to do exactly that, and in the next section we will examine the arguments he provides.

SIN AND PLANTINGA'S FREE WILL DEFENSE

Plantinga's free will defense is built on the principle that human beings can freely choose to sin and thereby cause evil to occur. Robert Adams and others have maintained that some sins are involuntary, and perhaps they are correct. But only a hard determinist would argue that the sins that human beings commit are never freely performed.

In this section I will present Plantinga's free will defense. Plantinga's articulation of the free will defense is quite complex and in some places difficult to comprehend, and for this reason I will rely on a simplified version provided by Paul Tidman.[1]

Tidman begins by stating, "Plantinga's free will defense achieved something fairly rare in philosophy—widespread consensus that it works" (Tidman 2008, 299). He quotes Peter Van Inwagen as saying, "It used to be widely held that evil . . . was incompatible with the existence of God:

that no possible world contained both God and evil. So far as I am able to tell, this thesis is no longer defended" (ibid.). Tidman credits the free will defense with causing this type of objection to theism to disappear.

Since it is a defense, Plantinga's work is not intended to explain why God permits evil. Since the time of Augustine theologians, clerics, rabbis, and pastors have advanced theories to explain why God permits evil. Today these theories are just that—theories. But Tidman notes that all one needs to do to rebut the deductive problem of evil is to prove that it is possible for two propositions both to be true: (1) An omnipotent and wholly good being exists, and (2) evil exists.

At the heart of the free will defense, Tidman observes, is the proposition that it is possible for a being who is omnipotent and perfectly good to create someone who has significant moral freedom and who makes use of this freedom by sinning and causing evil. By "significant moral freedom" Plantinga means the freedom to make morally significant choices, which includes the freedom to cause evil.

If it is possible for a being who is omnipotent and wholly good to create someone who has significant moral freedom and who freely sins and causes evil, it might appear that Plantinga has already shown that propositions 1 and 2 can both be true. However, the situation is more complicated than one might initially suppose. Mackie raises the possibility that an omnipotent God could create only beings who always freely choose the good, and if this is possible it is no longer clear that propositions 1 and 2 can both be true. God's moral goodness would, Mackie believes, require or constrain him to follow this path.

Responding to this point requires a fair amount of argumentation on Plantinga's part. Tidman observes that Plantinga's response proceeds along two lines. He first argues that the idea that God can bring about any possible world is mistaken. Some possible worlds cannot be actualized even by an omnipotent being. It has been widely believed that God can create any possible world he pleases, and the source of this widespread belief is Leibniz, according to Plantinga. He refers to this belief as "Leibniz Lapse."

To show that Leibniz is mistaken, Plantinga makes use of an example that does not involve sin or evil. Maurice is deciding whether or not to eat oatmeal, and let us assume that his decision is free. In one possible world, he decides to eat oatmeal. In another possible world, in exactly the same set of circumstances, he decides not to eat oatmeal. Depending on which decision Maurice makes, there is a possible world that not even God could have actualized. The world that becomes actualized is up to the free choice of Maurice, not God. If there is a possible world in which Maurice freely chooses to eat oatmeal, God cannot actualize a possible world (where Maurice is in exactly the same circumstances) in which he does not freely choose to eat oatmeal, and vice versa.

Through this stage of Plantinga's argumentation, sin and evil have not yet been addressed. Hence it has not yet been demonstrated that it is possible for an omnipotent and perfectly good being to create someone with significant moral freedom who uses this freedom by sinning and causing evil. Thus the second phase of Plantinga's response to Mackie is to show that it is possible that God could not have created a world in which everyone freely chooses what is right.

Recall from chapter 1 Plantinga's notion of transworld depravity. A moral agent suffers from transworld depravity, according to Tidman's formulation of Plantinga's definition, if the agent is such that, if he or she were created, he or she would go wrong with respect to at least one moral choice. Plantinga's strategy is to prove that it is possible that, no matter whom God created, this person would have sinned or performed at least some wrong actions.

Plantinga believes that a good example of someone who suffers from transworld depravity is James Curley, a former mayor of Boston. Whereas the choice of Maurice is not morally significant, Curley's freely choosing to accept a bribe is morally significant because it involved a sin of considerable magnitude. Because Curley's choice to accept a bribe was free, a possible world must have existed that was exactly like the world where he chose to accept the bribe (call these circumstances C), except that he turned down the bribe. Could God have actualized this world? The answer is that possibly he could not.

Here is why it might not even have been in God's power to actualize a world in which Curley refused the bribe. Before God decided which world to actualize, there was already a truth to the matter pertaining to Curley's choice. If God placed Curley in circumstances C, Curley would have chosen to take the bribe. Now we have seen that because Maurice's choice was free, there were worlds that God could not actualize, and the same is true here. Since Curley would have freely accepted the bribe in circumstances C, even God could not actualize a possible world in which Curley freely refused the bribe in circumstances C.

If for any possible world God might have actualized it is true that for at least one free choice Curley would have sinned in a morally significant manner, Curley suffered from transworld depravity. Moreover, Plantinga shows that if it is possible that Curley suffered from it, it is possible that every moral agent God might have created suffers from transworld depravity; this is the free will defense in a nutshell. If this is true, then it might not have been possible for God to create a world with moral good but no moral sin or evil.

Plantinga proceeds to demonstrate that if it is possible that every moral agent God has created suffers from transworld depravity, it is possible that anyone God might have created would have suffered from transworld depravity. From this it follows that it is possible that God could not have actualized a possible world with significant moral good but no significant moral evil. The demise of the deductive problem of evil is the direct result of Plantinga's proving that this state of affairs is possible. The deductive problem of evil no longer has serious defenders in the philosophical realm.

Let us now summarize the conclusions of this section. The deductive problem of evil states that a wholly good, omnipotent being does not allow evil to exist. All one needs to do to rebut the deductive problem of evil is to show that it is possible for both of the following propositions to be true: (1) An omnipotent and wholly good being exists, and (2) evil exists.

Plantinga embraces the principle that human beings with significant moral freedom can make use of their freedom by sinning and bringing about moral evil. Mackie, however, argues that an omnipotent God could create beings who freely choose the good and that God's moral goodness would require him to actualize a world containing only such beings.

Plantinga goes on to argue that some possible worlds cannot be actualized, even by God. If Maurice freely chooses to eat oatmeal in some possible world, God cannot actualize a world in which Maurice is in exactly the same circumstances in which he doesn't freely choose to eat oatmeal. The same line of reasoning applies to Curley's free choice to accept a bribe. From here Plantinga introduces the notion of transworld depravity. Curley suffered from transworld depravity because he would have sinned in a morally significant manner in any world God might have actualized. And if this is true, Plantinga argues, it is possible that every moral agent God might have created would have suffered from transworld depravity. This shows, finally, that it might not have been possible for God to create a world with moral good but no moral evil.

CONCLUSION

The key role that sin plays in Plantinga's free will defense has perhaps been underappreciated in the literature on the problem of evil (in other contexts, Plantinga has spoken at length about the pervasive presence of sin in the universe; see, for example, his views concerning the noetic effects of sin in chapter 1).

Other philosophers who have addressed this topic have been quite mindful of sin's relevance. Marilyn Adams, in her essay "Horrendous Evils and the Goodness of God," offers a list of ghastly sins that might incline one to be skeptical of God's goodness:

> The rape of a woman and axing off of her arms, psychophysical torture whose ultimate goal is the disintegration of personality, betrayal of one's deepest loyalties, cannibalism of one's own offspring, child abuse of the sort described by Ivan Karamazov, child pornography, parental incest, slow death by starvation, participation in the Nazi death camps, the explosion of nuclear bombs over populated areas, having to choose which of one's children should live and which to be executed by terrorists, being the accidental and/or unwitting agent of the disfigurement or death of those one loves best. (Adams 2008, 316)

Against the backdrop of Adams's discussion, it is beyond obvious that the topic of sin figures prominently in the problem of evil.[2]

CHAPTER TEN

SIN IN SIX MAJOR
WORLD RELIGIONS

The concept of sin is understood in a variety of ways by different world religions. In the first section of this chapter, I will briefly examine the teachings of six major religions: Catholicism, Hinduism, Islam, Judaism, Orthodoxy, and Protestantism. In the second section of this chapter I will present more expansive comments on these teachings against the backdrop of the previous nine chapters. The third section will consist of concluding comments, not just for this chapter but for the book as a whole.

Naturally, because of space limitations, the presentations of the teachings of these world religions will be briefer than one might desire and, in some cases, slightly oversimplified.[1] I will not discuss Buddhism because Buddhist thought has no concept of sin that is comparable to what is understood by the other six religions included here.

SIN IN THE MAJOR WORLD RELIGIONS

The Catholic Church defines sin as an offense against reason, truth, and right conscience. It is a failure in genuine love for God and neighbor caused by a perverse attachment to certain goods. Sin is an offense against God. It sets itself against God's love for us and turns our hearts away from it. Like the first sin, it is disobedience, a revolt against God through the prideful will to become like God. In this proud self-exaltation, sin is diametrically opposed to obedience to Jesus.

Here sin is characterized as an offense against God, disobedience to God (unlike the obedience of Jesus), and a revolt against God. It is also described as an offense against reason, truth, and conscience, implying that human beings can identify the truth about what is sinful both through reason and through conscience. Sin is caused by perverse attachments to certain goods and also by human beings' desire to become like God. As we saw in chapter 4, Catholicism acknowledges a distinction between mortal sin and venial sin. Catholics affirm the teachings of the Bible, both the Old and New Testaments, and a set of books known as the Apocrypha, and their views on sin are shaped by teachings in all of these.

Hinduism views sin not as a crime against God but as an act against dharma, moral order, and one's own self. When souls act wrongly, they are living in nescience, the darkness of ignorance. Sin is an adharmic course of action that automatically brings negative consequences. The term "sin" in Hinduism actually carries a double meaning: (1) a wrongful act and (2) the negative consequences resulting from a wrongful act.

Several points are worthy of comment. First, the teaching that souls acting wrongly are living in nescience is an epistemological teaching. This teaching suggests that illumination, or the absence of ignorance, can function as an antidote to sin. In other words, knowledge of the proper kind can lead in the direction of avoiding sin. Second, Hinduism recognizes that one can sin against one's own self. While this teaching might initially strike one as dubious, reflection might render it more plausible. Nevertheless, finding examples of this phenomenon that are universally convincing might be difficult (more on this in the next section). Third, Hinduism regards the negative consequences resulting from a wrongful act as sins. This is certainly an intriguing idea, one that involves the notion of causation. More about this will be said in the next section.

Judaism teaches that human beings are not inherently sinful. We come into the world neither carrying the burden of sin committed by our ancestors nor tainted by it. Sin, *het*, is the result of our human inclinations, which must be properly channeled. *Het* literally means something that goes astray. This concept of sin suggests a straying from the correct ways, from what is good and straight. Humans can be absolved of their failure. The narratives of the books of Moses establish the concept of the God of Israel as a God of mercy and forgiveness. In rabbinic Judaism these ideas evolved into the idea that God has the attributes of both justice and mercy, the latter of which is the dominant mode of God's authority.

Here we find a rejection of the doctrine of original sin so forceful that it stipulates that we are not even tainted by the sins of our ancestors (recall the discussions of taint in earlier chapters). Typically one who rejects the idea of original sin argues that we are in no way responsible for the sins of our ancestors or, more specifically, the first human beings. To say that we are not even tainted by their sins is a stronger claim, and that is what Judaism teaches. Nevertheless, we possess human inclinations that can lead to sin. It is also noteworthy that in Judaism humans can be absolved of their failure to do what is good due to the mercy of God (Judaism acknowledges the historical Jesus but not, of course, the divinity of Jesus). Forgiveness comes from God the father.

Muslims believe that people are born in a state of intrinsic goodness. Like Adam, people are born pure and sinless. They are Muslims by birth, their salvation is intact, and they must do all in their power to maintain this status. Unfortunately, maintaining a sinless life in the long run is impossible. Humans become sinful due to outside influences. Muslims reject the doctrine of original sin. Nothing is right or wrong by nature, but it becomes such by the fiat of the Almighty. What Allah forbids is sin even when He forbids what seems to human conscience right and lawful.

An emphatic rejection of the doctrine of original sin is linked to a belief in the intrinsic goodness of human beings (a belief held by Rousseau for very different reasons). The Muslim belief that right and wrong are determined solely by a fiat of the Almighty is a teaching that is not far removed from the divine command theory of morality (more on this in the next section). And Muslims believe that human conscience can err in distinguishing between right and wrong, a teaching that seems on the face of it quite plausible.

In the Orthodox Church there are no categories of sin. There is no distinction between mortal and venial sins, for example. The target toward which one aims is a Christlike life, one lived to the best of one's ability in line with the teachings and commandments of God. When one misses this target, one sins. It makes no difference if one misses by an inch or a yard. In both cases missing counts as a sin.

The most prominent feature of this account is the teaching that there is no distinction between sins of great magnitude and sins of lesser magnitude. Thus, what one might be tempted to characterize as a sin of minimal importance is in reality a sin no different in magnitude from any other sin. Also noteworthy is the teaching that the target at which one aims is living to the best of one's ability in line with the teachings and commandments of God. Here is an apparent recognition of the fact, discussed in chapter 6, that God expresses his will concerning one's actions in ways other than his commandments (more on this point in the next section).

Protestants believe that God created people good, in true righteousness and holiness. The disobedience of Adam and Eve, their fall from righteousness, has poisoned human nature in such a way that all are born sinners. Human beings are corrupt from conception on, unable to do any good and inclined to all evil, unless they are "born again." Since God created humans good, he has not done them any injustice. God is merciful, but he is also just. Hence, disobedience and rebellion cannot go unpunished.

The doctrine of the fall from righteousness is a central component of Protestantism. Like adherents to some of the other world religions, Protestants affirm that human beings are created good. But by the time they are born they are sinners due to the disobedience of Adam and Eve. Hence they place a strong, unmistakable emphasis on the Augustinian doctrine of original sin. Protestants stress the need for human beings to be born again in spirit, and the ability to be born again is a result of God's mercy (through the atonement of Jesus Christ). Protestants affirm the teachings of the Bible, both the Old and New Testaments, but different Protestant denominations differ on how passages of Scripture are to be interpreted, including passages dealing with the topic of sin.

ADDITIONAL COMMENTS ON THESE TEACHINGS

Having surveyed the views of six major world religions concerning sin, I will comment on some of these teachings against the backdrop of the previous chapters (I use the term "backdrop" somewhat loosely; not all of the material covered in this section relates directly to topics found in the previous chapters). Topics to be discussed in this section are the doctrine of original sin, the claim that one can sin against one's own self, the claim that the negative consequences resulting from a wrongful act are themselves sins, the view that life ought to be lived in accord with both God's teachings and his commandments, and the teaching that nothing is right or wrong by nature but becomes such by the fiat of the Almighty.

First I will address the topic of original sin, which was the topic of chapter 1. As seen above, Judaism and Islam emphatically reject the doctrine of original sin. Judaism goes so far as to teach that human beings are not even tainted by the sins of their ancestors. Hinduism does not view sin as a crime against God, and hence there is no room for a doctrine of original sin, at least along Augustinian lines.

Protestantism offers a congenial conceptual setting for the doctrine of original sin due to its heavy emphasis on humans' fall from righteousness. Protestantism teaches that the reason human beings have fallen from righteousness is that Adam and Eve sinned against God. This is the classic Augustinian view of original sin.

Hinduism teaches that one can sin against one's own self, and it is possible that some of the other major world religions would concur. Is this a plausible view regarding sin? Initially one might be skeptical, but suppose that it is possible to make promises to one's own self. For instance, suppose that I promise myself never to become a habitual user of drugs. I make this promise because I foresee that doing so would have a deleterious effect on my health and my relationships with others. Subsequently I break the promise and become a habitual user of drugs. Here it is reasonable to judge that I have sinned against myself. Not everyone might agree that this particular example is an instance of sinning against one's own self, but I believe that the teaching that it is possible to sin against one's own self is widely accepted.

Hinduism regards the negative consequences resulting from a wrongful act as sins. If I sin by striking another person, the injury to that person is a sin attributable to me. And if that person receives costly medical treatment for the injury, that is also a sin attributable to me. It is not clear how long the causal chain becomes before the sin is no longer attributable to me. Surely this idea runs counter to the ways people ordinarily speak about sin. Ordinarily a sinful act is regarded as one thing and the negative consequences, though regarded as results for which one is likely to be morally responsible, are not themselves regarded as additional sins. Nevertheless, one who takes this teaching seriously may be less likely to commit the first sin in a causal chain that could conceivably be lengthy. In other words, this teaching could constitute a deterrent to sinning.

Orthodoxy teaches that the target toward which one aims is a life lived to the best of one's abilities in line with the teachings and commandments of God. I believe this statement is significant by virtue of acknowledging both the teachings of God and the commandments of God. In chapter 6, I made a distinction between the commandments of God and the counsels of God. I said that it is optional to follow the counsels of God, and responding to them in a spirit of liberty is appropriate. Moreover, God intends his counsels to benefit those who act in accord with them. To the extent that God's counsels can be regarded as teachings of God (though only a subset of his teachings), the fact that Orthodoxy acknowledges both the teachings of God and his commandments is arguably a significant point.

Muslims believe that nothing is right or wrong by nature; actions become such by the fiat of the Almighty. The divine command theory of morality, roughly speaking, states that morally wrong actions are determined by what violates the commands of God, and actions that do not violate these commands are morally permissible. These respective teachings appear to be very similar. Muslims believe that if an action is wrong, it is wrong by virtue of the fiat of the Almighty. Those subscribing to the divine command theory of morality believe that if something is wrong, it is wrong by virtue of violating a command of God. Some may wish to argue that fiats and commands are not entirely the same, and no doubt they are correct; nevertheless, there is a definite similarity between the teachings of Muslims regarding what determines whether something is wrong and the corresponding beliefs of those defending the divine command theory of morality.

CONCLUSION

In this book I have acknowledged a distinction between sin understood as a pervasive, inescapable feature of the human condition and the individual sins committed by human beings. The doctrine of original sin describes the manner in which sin has become a pervasive, inescapable feature of the human condition, and this was the subject matter of chapter 1. Most of the subsequent chapters, in one way or another, were concerned with the individual sins committed by human moral agents. Chapter 2 broadened this theme to explore the possibility of sins performed by collectives of human moral agents and the possibility of collectives' bearing guilt for these sins.

The next two chapters address the topics of accessory sins, mortal versus venial sins, the thesis that some sins are more serious than others from a moral perspective, and the seven deadly sins. The main lessons to be learned from these two chapters are that it can be sinful to become complicit in the wrongful actions of others and that not all sins are the same. Some are more serious than others, or so I have argued.

Chapters 5 and 6 complement each other in a certain sense. Chapter 5 concerns acts of supererogation, acts that one is praiseworthy to perform but are not obligatory (and one is not blameworthy to omit performing them). Chapter 6 deals with acts that are the mirror image of these supererogatory acts, namely, acts that humans are blameworthy to perform but are not obligatory, acts that seem to capture the spirit of acts that are classified as discouraged in Islamic ethics.

The main lessons to be learned from these two chapters are as follows. First, even though human beings are sinful and even if the doctrine of original sin is true, it is possible for people to go beyond the call of duty. Second, it can at times be sinful to refrain from going beyond the call of duty. Third, under certain circumstances it can be sinful to perform actions that are discouraged but not outright forbidden.

Chapter 7 contains an account of moral ideals and an explanation of how moral ideals differ from moral virtues. Here sin can take the form of the failure to develop moral virtue, the intent to develop moral vice, and the outright practice of moral vice. The symbolic dimension of sin is the subject matter of chapter 8. Inspired by the work of Robert Nozick (1993), the notion of the symbolic value of an act can be characterized as follows: The performance of one act can symbolize the performance of other actual or potential acts or the bringing about of certain states of affairs in a manner that has moral significance.

Thus, the performance of a sinful act can symbolize the performance of a different sinful act, a sinful omission can symbolize a different sinful omission, and so forth. Chapter 9 explores the relationship between sin and evil by analyzing the deductive problem of evil and the role sin plays in demonstrating that it is not a genuine problem for theists. The present chapter contains an examination of how the concept of sin is understood by the major world religions.

Doubtless, there are people who do not acknowledge that sin is something real, and perhaps there are people who affirm that sin is something real but also believe that our knowledge of what is sinful is so inadequate that theorizing about it is beyond our capacity. In this treatment of the relationship between sin and moral wrongdoing I have assumed that sin is a feature of human life and experience that is real and undeniable. I have also assumed that our knowledge of what is sinful versus what is not sinful, though subject to error, is not so limited as to preclude our applying philosophical concepts and categories to our understanding of it.

I do not claim to have covered every issue concerning sin that is capable of being shown to have philosophical significance. My choice of topics was largely the result of issues thought to be significant by philosophers who have written about sin. Those who can identify additional areas in which light can be shed on the nature of sin by way of philosophical analysis will be in a position to enlighten the philosophical community. The treatment of the relationship between sin and moral wrongdoing provided here can be regarded as an initial step in a process that will perhaps be ongoing.

NOTES

CHAPTER FOUR. Mortal versus Venial Sins

1. More will be said about this point in chapter 10.

2. For Aquinas, capital vices can also have mortal and venial forms, but capital vices are not the same as mortal sins.

3. Scripture speaks of an unforgivable sin, blasphemy against the Holy Spirit, in Mark 3:29.

4. William Mann describes the thesis that all sins are equal as a notorious Stoic thesis (Mann 1999, 158).

5. Plantinga clearly believes that sins can vary according to degrees of badness, but it is not clear whether he acknowledges that sins can vary according to degrees of wrongness. To me it seems clear that sins can vary according to degrees of both badness and wrongness, and this understanding will serve as the basis of my illustrations.

CHAPTER FIVE. Supererogation and Sin

1. Not everyone who denies the possibility of supererogation for human moral agents is committed to the denial of the ought-implies-can principle. See, for example, the system described by Fred Feldman in *Doing the Best We Can* (1986).

2. In general, the term "deontic" refers roughly to the contrast between right and wrong, and the term "aretaic" refers to the contrast between virtue and vice.

CHAPTER SEVEN.   Moral Ideas, Virtue Ethics, and Sin

1. One or two writers have been skeptical of following Aristotle in regarding moral virtues as dispositions. An example is Robert Adams in *A Theory of Virtue* (2006).

CHAPTER EIGHT.   Sin and Symbolism

1. According to Marilyn McCord Adams, Anselm treats sin "primarily as a category of (negative) symbolic value" (Adams 1999, 98).

CHAPTER NINE.   Sin and the Probem of Evil

1. Tidman's simplified version is not entirely accurate, as an anonymous reader has pointed out, but for our present purposes it will prove reliable.

2. It might appear that what Adams has in mind here is the probabilistic problem of evil rather than the deductive problem of evil, but her remarks are made squarely in the context of discussing Mackie's argument.

CHAPTER TEN.   Sin in Six Major World Religions

1. The sources for this chapter are as follows: Catholicism—*Catechism of the Catholic Church*, 2nd ed. (Washington, DC: United States Conference of Catholic Bishops, 2019), Part 3, sect. 1, chap. 1, art. 8; Hinduism—Satguru Sivaya Subramuniyaswami (Master), *Loving Gaesa: Hinduism's Endearing Elephant-Faced God*, (Master) (Malaysia: Sampoorna Printers SDN BHD by arrangement with Uma Publications, 2000), p. 679; Judaism—Rabbi Dr. Reuven Hammer, *The Jewish View of Sin*, myjewishlearning.com; Islam—xemercenter.com; Orthodoxy—oca.org/question/sacramentconfession/sin; Protestantism—Louis Berkhof, *Manual of Christian Doctrine* (Arlington Heights, IL: Christian Liberty Press).

BIBLIOGRAPHY

Adams, Marilyn McCord. 1999. "Romancing the Good." In *The Augustinian Tradition*, ed. Gareth B. Matthews. Berkeley: University of California Press, 91–109.

———. 2002. "Neglected Values, Shrunken Agents, Happy Endings: A Reply to Rogers." *Faith and Philosophy* 19, no. 2: 214–232.

———. 2008. "Horrendous Evils and the Goodness of God." In *Readings in the Philosophy of Religion*, ed. Kelly James Clark, 2nd ed. Buffalo, NY: Broadview, 315–322.

Adams, Robert Merrihew. 1985. "Involuntary Sins." *Philosophical Review* 94, no. 1: 3–31.

———. 1987. *The Virtue of Faith*. Oxford: Oxford University Press.

———. 2006. *A Theory of Virtue*. Oxford: Oxford University Press.

Allen, Joseph. 1984. *Love and Conflict*. Nashville: Abingdon.

Andrade, Gabriel. 2014. "Rene Girard." In *Internet Encyclopedia of Philosophy*. https://iep.utm.edu/girard/.

Annas, Julia. 2011. *Intelligent Virtue*. Oxford: Oxford University Press.

Appiah, Anthony. 1991. "Racism and Moral Pollution." In *Collective Responsibility*, ed. Larry May and Stacey Hoffman. Savage, MD: Rowman and Littlefield.

Aquinas, Thomas. 1894. *Summa Theologia*. Turin: P. Marietti.

Audi, Robert. 2005. "Wrongs within Rights." In *Normativity*, ed. Ernest Sosa and Enrique Villanueva. Boston: Blackwell, 121–139.

Augustine. 1948. "The Confessions." In *Basic Writings of Saint Augustine*, vol. 1, ed. Whitney J. Oates. New York: Random House, 3–256.

Beauchamp, Tom. 1995. "Moral Ideals." In *The Oxford Companion to Philosophy*, ed. T. Honderich. Oxford: Oxford University Press, 388ff.

Brandt, Richard. 1963. "Toward a Credible Form of Utilitarianism." In *Morality and the Language of Conduct*, ed. Hector-Neri Casteneda and George N. Nakhnikian. Detroit: Wayne State University Press, 107–143.

———. 1971. "Some Merits of One Form of Rule Utilitarianism." In *Mill: Utilitarianism with Critical Essays*, ed. Samuel Gorovitz. Indianapolis: Bobbs-Merrill, 324–344.

Calvin, John. 1960. *Institutes of the Christian Religion*, ed. John T. McNeill, trans. Ford Lewis Battles. Philadelphia: Westminster Press.

Chisholm, Roderick, and Ernest Sosa. 1966. "Intrinsic Preferability and the Problem of Supererogation." *Synthese* 16: 321–331.

Couenhoven, Jesse. 2013. *Stricken by Sin, Cured by Christ*. Oxford: Oxford University Press.

Crisp, Oliver D. 2015. "On Original Sin." *International Journal of Systematic Theology* 17, no. 3: 252–266.

Cuneo, Terence. 1994. "Combating the Noetic Effects of Sin: Pascal's Strategy for Natural Theology." *Faith and Philosophy* 11, no. 4: 645–662.

De Marco, Joseph. 1995. *Moral Theory*. London: Jones and Bartlett.

DeYoung, Rebecca Konyndyk. 2008. "The Seven Deadly Sins." In *The Encyclopedia of Christianity*, vol. 5, ed. Geoffrey W. Bromily. Boston, MA: Brill, 25–26.

———. 2009. *Glittering Vices: A New Look at the Seven Deadly Sins and Their Remedies*. Grand Rapids, MI: Brazos.

Driver, Julia. 1992. "The Suberogatory." *Australasian Journal of Philosophy* 70: 286–293.

Edwards, Jonathan. 1970. *Original Sin*, ed. Clyde A. Holbrook. New Haven, CT: Yale University Press.

Evagrius of Pontus. 2003. *The Greek Ascetic Corpus*, trans. R. E. Sinkewicz. London, Oxford University Press.

Feldman, Fred. 1986. *Doing the Best We Can*. Dordrecht, Netherlands: D. Reidel.

Frankena, William. 1963. *Ethics*. Englewood Cliffs, NJ: Prentice-Hall.

Garrett, Thomas. 1966. *Business Ethics*. Englewood Cliffs, NJ: Prentice-Hall.

Gert, Bernard. 2004. *Common Morality*. New York: Oxford University Press.

Gilkey, Langdon. 1966. *Shanting Compound*. New York: Harper and Row.

Gregory the Great. 1844. *Morals on the Book of Job*, trans. John Henry Parker and J. Rivington. London, Oxford University Press.

Hare, John. 1996. *The Moral Gap*. Oxford: Clarendon Press.

Hare, R. M. 1969. *Freedom and Reason*. London: Oxford University Press.

Hume, David. 1948. *Dialogues Concerning Natural Religion*, ed. Norman Kemp Smith. New York: Social Science Publishers.

Kant, Immanuel. 1960. *Religion within the Limits of Reason.* New York: Harper & Row.

Langerak, Edward. 2014. *Civil Disagreement.* Washington, DC: Georgetown University Press.

Leibniz, Gottfried Wilhelm. 1699. *Confessio Philosophi*, ed. Otto Saame. Frankfurt: Vittorio Klostermann.

Lewis, H. D. 1948. "Collective Responsibility." *Philosophy* 23: 3–18.

Luther, Martin. 1943. "Treatise on Good Works." In *Works of Martin Luther*. Philadelphia: Muhlenberg Press.

MacDonald, Scott. 1999. "Primal Sin." In *The Augustinian Tradition*, ed. Gareth Matthews. Berkeley, CA: University of California Press, 110–139.

Mackie, J. L. 1955. "Evil and Omnipotence." *Mind* 64, 200ff.

MacIntyre, Alasdair. 1981. *After Virtue.* Notre Dame, IN: University of Notre Dame Press.

Mann, William E. 1999. "Inner-Life Ethics." In *The Augustinian Tradition*, ed. Gareth B. Matthews. Berkelely: University of California Press, 140–165.

May, Larry. 1992. *Sharing Responsibility.* Chicago: University of Chicago Press.

Melanchton, Philip. 1969. *Loci Communes Theologi*, ed. Wilhelm Pauck. Philadelphia: Westminster Press.

Mellema, Gregory. 1995. "Sin." In *Oxford Companion to Philosophy*, ed. Ted Honderich. Oxford: Oxford University Press.

———. 1998. *Collective Responsibility.* Amsterdam: Rodopi.

———. 1999. "Symbolic Value, Virtue Ethics, and the Morality of Groups." *Philosophy Today* 43: 302–309.

———. 2000. "Scapegoats." In *Criminal Justice Ethics* 19: 3–9.

———. 2010. "Moral Ideals and Virtue Ethics." *Journal of Ethics* 14: 173–180.

———. 2016. *Complicity and Moral Accountability.* Notre Dame, IN: University of Notre Dame Press.

Mill, John Stuart. 1907. *Utilitarianism.* London: Longmans, Green.

Moroney, Stephen K. 2000. *The Noetic Effects of Sin.* Lanham, MD: Lexington.

New, Christopher. 1974. "Saints, Heroes, and Utilitarians." *Philosophy* 49: 179–189.

Newhauser, Richard. 1993. *The Treatise on Vices and Virtues in Latin and the Vernacular.* Turnhout, Belgium: Brepols.

Nozick, Robert. 1993. *The Nature of Rationality.* New York: Harper and Row.

Ott, Ludwig. 1955. *Fundamentals of Catholic Dogma*, ed. James Canon Bastible. Rockford, IL: Tan Books and Publishers.

Pascal, Blaise. 1966. *Pensees*, trans. A. J. Krailsheimer. New York: Penguin.

Pawl, Timothy, and Kevin Timpe. 2009. "Incompatibilism, Sin, and Free Will in Heaven." *Faith and Philosophy* 26, 396–417.

Plantinga, Alvin. 1974. *God, Freedom, and Evil.* Grand Rapids, MI: Eerdmans.

———. 2000. *Warranted Christian Belief.* New York: Oxford University Press.

Plantinga, Cornelius. 1995. *Not the Way It's Supposed to Be: A Breviary of Sin.* Grand Rapids, MI: William Eerdmans.

Pybus, Elizabeth. 1982. "Saints and Heroes." *Philosophy* 57, 193–199.

Quinn, Philip. 1990. "Does Anxiety Explain Original Sin?" *Nous* 24 no. 2: 227–244.

Rahner, Karl. 1965. "The Theology of the Religious Life." In *Religious Orders in the Modern World,* ed. Gerard Huyghe et al. Westminster, MD: Newman.

Rea, Michael. 2007. "The Metaphysics of Original Sin." In *Persons Human and Divine,* ed. Dean Zimmerman and Peter Van Inwagen. New York: Oxford University Press, 319–356.

Ricoeur, Paul. 1967. *The Symbolism of Evil.* New York: Harper and Row.

Rogers, Katherin. 2002. "The Abolition of Sin: A Response to Adams in the Augustinian Tradition." *Faith and Philosophy* 19, no. 2: 69–84.

Ross, Sir David. 1973. *The Right and the Good.* London: Oxford University Press.

Ruse, Michael. 2001. *Can a Darwinian Be a Christian?* Cambridge: Cambridge University Press.

Sidgwick, Henry. 1981. *The Methods of Ethics,* 7th ed. Cambridge: Hackett.

Slote, Michael. 1983. *Goods and Virtues.* Oxford: Oxford University Press.

———. 1992. *From Morality to Virtue.* Oxford: Oxford University Press.

Stump, Eleonore. 1985. "The Problem of Evil." *Faith and Philosophy* 2, no. 4: 392–423.

———. 1988. "Atonement According to Aquinas." In *Philosophy and the Christian Faith,* ed. Thomas V. Morris. Notre Dame, IN: University of Notre Dame Press, 61–91.

Sverdlik, Steven. 1987. "Collective Responsibility." *Philosophical Studies* 51: 51–76.

Swinburne, Richard. 1988. "The Christian Scheme of Salvation." In *Philosophy and the Christian Faith,* ed. Thomas V. Morris. Notre Dame, IN: University of Notre Dame Press, 15–30.

———. 1989. *Responsibility and Atonement.* Oxford: Clarendon.

Taylor, Charles. 2007. *A Secular Age.* Cambridge, MA: Harvard University Press.

Thomson, Judith Jarvis. 1989. "Morality and Bad Luck." *Metaphilosophy* 20: 204ff.

Tidman, Paul. 2008. "The Free Will Defense." In *Readings in the Philosophy of Religion,* ed. Kelly James Clark, 2nd ed. Buffalo, NY: Broadview Press, 399–409.

Trianosky, Gregory. 1989. "Supererogation, Wrongdoing, and Vice: On the Autonomy of the Ethics of Virtue." *Journal of Philosophy* 83, 26ff.

Urmson, J. O. 1969. "Saints and Heroes." In *Moral Concepts*, ed. Joel Feinberg. London: Oxford University Press, 60–73.

Wainwright, William J. 1988. "Original Sin." In *Philosophy and the Christian Faith*, ed. Thomas V. Morris. Notre Dame, IN: University of Notre Dame Press, 31–60.

Wierenga, Edward. 2016. *The Philosophy of Religion*. Malden, MA: Wiley Blackwell.

INDEX

accomplices, 21–29
Adam, 1–4, 6–9, 98
Adams, Marilyn, 9, 94, 104
Adams, Robert, 6, 90, 104
Annas, Julia, 68
Anselm, Saint, 104
Appiah, Anthony, 25, 82
Aquinas, Thomas, 5, 13, 21–22, 32, 57,
    59–60
Arendt, Hannah, 19–20
Aristotle, 65
atonement, 14
Audi, Robert, 66–67, 70
Augustine, Saint, 2, 8, 13, 91

Belgic Confession, 9, 46
Benjamin, Martin, 16
blameworthy acts, 11–12, 14, 41–42,
    48–49, 51, 55, 57
Brandt, Richard, 66

Calvin, John, 43
Catholicism, Roman, 4, 31–33, 42,
    95–96
character traits, 68–69
collective
    guilt, 16, 18–19,80

inaction, 20
    responsibility, 16–18, 80–81
    sins, 18
commands, 21, 24, 27, 53–54, 57–58,
    100
compassion, 64
complicity, 21–26, 28–29
consent, 24, 27
contributing acts, 21, 81
Cooper, D. E., 17
corporations, 83
Couenhoven, Jesse, 2, 5
counsel, 24, 27, 57–60, 100
courage, 65

DeYoung, Rebecca Konyndyk, 38
discouraged acts, 53–62
dispositions, 68
Driver, Julia, 54–55
Duns Scotus, 2

Epicurus, 87
Eve, 1–2, 6–8, 98
evil, 33–34, 87–94
evolutionary theory, 3
existentialism, 19
expectation, moral, 56–57, 60

Feldman, Fred, 44, 103
forbidden acts, 12, 53–55, 58, 60–62
Frankena, William, 64–68
free will, 3, 10
French, Peter, 17

Gert, Bernard, 66
Gilkey, Langdon, 3
Gregory the Great, 38
guilt, 11–12, 14–15, 25

Hare, R. M., 65–66
heaven, 52
Heidelberg Catechism, 10, 46
Held, Virginia, 17
hell, 3
Hinduism, 96–99
Holocaust, 19, 25
Hume, David, 87

ideals, moral, 63–71
ignorance, 33
Islam, 35, 53–54, 57–62, 97, 99–100

Jaspers, Karl, 19
Jesus, 2
Judaism, 96–97, 99

Kant, Immanuel, 2, 29, 66–67

Leibniz, Gottfried Wilhelm, 6–7, 91
Lewis, H. D., 16–17
liberty, 59
Luther, Martin, 43

MacDonald, Scott, 8
MacIntyre, Alasdair, 77
Mackie, J. L., 87–91
Mann, William, 103
May, Larry, 17, 19–20
Melanchthon, Philip, 43
Miller, Suemas, 16

moral climate, 83
moral luck, 28–30

Narveson, Jan, 16
New, Christopher, 44
Newhauser, Richard, 21
Niebuhr, Reinhold, 3
noetic effects, 5
Nozick, Robert, 73–76, 79

obligations, moral, 11–12, 41
offences, 12, 55
Old Testament, 60
omnipotence, 88–89, 91, 93
Orthodoxy, 4, 97–98, 100
ought-implies-can principle, 45

Pascal, Blaise, 5
permitted acts, 55
Plantinga, Alvin, 5–6, 10, 90–94
Plantinga, Cornelius, 13, 34–36, 63, 103
Plato, 64–65, 70
Ponticus, Evagrius, 38
praiseworthy acts, 41, 45, 47, 51–52
pride, 38–39
principal actors, 21, 26–27, 29
promising, practice of, 74–75
Protestantism, 98–99
Pybus, Elizabeth, 66

quasi–supererogation, 50–51
Quinn, Philip, 2

Rahner, Karl, 43
Rea, Michael, 2, 7–8
recommended acts, 53, 58
Ricoeur, Paul, 82
Ross, Sir David, 44
Ruse, Michael, 4

sacrificial lamb, 15
Sartre, Jean–Paul, 19

scapegoats, 14–15, 78–79
Second Helvetic Confession, 35
shalom, 13
shame, 15, 20
Sidgwick, Henry, 66
silence, 28
sins
  accessory, 21–30
  ancestral, 4
  gradations of, 35
  inherited, 2
  mortal, 31–34
  original, 1–5, 45, 47, 97–99
  primal, 8
  seven deadly, 38
  symbolism of, 73–85
  venial, 31–34
Slote, Michael, 66
Stump, Eleonore, 3
suberogatory acts, 54–55
supererogation, 41–52

Sverdlik, Steven, 16–17
Swinburne, Richard, 13, 33
symbolic value, 74–85

taint, moral, 7–8, 25–26, 82
Taylor, Charles, 64
Ten Commandments, 32
Tetzel, Johann, 42
Thomson, Judith Jarvis, 28
Tidman, Paul, 10, 90–91
total depravity, 9, 46
Trianosky, Gregory, 48–49

uncleanness, 9
Urmson, J. O., 43, 46
utilitarianism, 44

Van Inwagen, Peter, 90
vices, 39, 49–50, 70–71, 76–78
virtues, 39, 63, 67–71, 76–78

Gregory Mellema is professor emeritus of philosophy at Calvin University. Among other books, he is the author of *Complicity and Moral Accountability* (University of Notre Dame Press, 2016, 2021).

9 780268 201333